Please feel free to photocopy this material to share with your friends and colleagues. You are welcome to use any information as long as you include a note acknowledging the source.

The Economic Situation of Women Over 55, Present and Projected

June 1994

ISBN 0-7732-1382-1

A discussion paper prepared for the
Alberta Advisory Council on Women's Issues

by

Donna Kerr
Kerr Creative Consulting
Edmonton, Alberta

TABLE OF CONTENTS

RECOMMENDATIONS

The Alberta Advisory Council on Women's Issues believes that until women have achieved economic equality, they will not be able to achieve full and equal participation in Alberta society. In addition, women must be **active** partners in decision-making processes at all levels.

The structure of our society has ensured that women as a group are in poor shape economically. This is particularly evident in the examination of the economic situation of women over 55.

The solutions to the problems related to women's economic status in Alberta do not lie solely with government. Governments, communities, employers, educators, and individuals must work together in achieving the economic equality of women.

Therefore, in formulating recommendations on this subject, the Alberta Advisory Council on Women's Issues has included four sets of recommendations: action steps the Government of Alberta might take and those which might be undertaken by the community at large, as well as the business community and by women themselves.

RECOMMENDATIONS TO THE GOVERNMENT OF ALBERTA

Whereas:

Training and education are the keys to better jobs and resulting economic independence.

Whereas:

Current training and education programs may reinforce systemic discrimination and the ghettoization of women's work.

Whereas:

The Ministry of Education is currently reviewing the Career and Life Management Program (CALM).

The Alberta Advisory Council on Women's Issues recommends that:

The Government of Alberta identify the number and type of jobs in job-creation programs, and the number of women employed as a result of these programs.

and

Ensure that training dollars for women are directed to programs that will provide marketable skills for long-term employment that will help to assure sustainable economic independence.

and

The Government of Alberta implement combined high-school upgrading/apprenticeship programs to meet the need for in-demand trades, and that women be encouraged to participate in these programs.

and

Ensure clear sexual harassment policies and procedures in such programs are in place and are enforced.

and

Ensure the Career and Life Management Program (CALM) includes education on practical financial issues and be representative of women's lives and economic realities.

and

The regulations of the Student Finance Board be reviewed and revised to ensure single parents' access to schooling that will lead to long-term employment that pays sufficient income to assure sustainable economic independence.

and

The Ministry of Advanced Education and Career Development ensure education and training programs being accessed by single parents reflect policies of flexibility such as part-time attendance and alternative delivery modes, to allow for dependent care responsibilities.

Whereas:

In economics, consumers and persons aren't counted—households are, which results in the masking of women's personal poverty.

The "household" and the thinking behind it serve as a background to theories of income distribution, taxation, welfare, and economic development. Formulation of government policy is currently based (using Census data) on measures of household income and therefore does not adequately represent the economic status of women as individuals.

The Alberta Advisory Council on Women's Issues recommends that:

The Government of Alberta formulate policy on women's individual economic condition.

and

The Government of Alberta formally request the Government of Canada to include women's unpaid work in the calculation of the Gross Domestic Product.

and

The Government of Alberta formally request the Government of Canada to begin the process of determining policy based on women's individual economic condition.

Whereas:

The language of economics is unfamiliar to many women and further marginalizes their literate participation in understanding and working to develop policies that may have a positive outcome in their lives.

The Alberta Advisory Council on Women's Issues recommends that:

The Government of Alberta work in partnership with its relevant agencies and financial institutions to develop written and video educational materials in plain language to improve women's economic literacy.

and

Government economic policy be written in plain language.

RECOMMENDATIONS FOR THE COMMUNITY

Whereas:

Adequate, affordable housing is a basis of economic security; and home ownership by women is a step towards economic security.

The Alberta Advisory Council on Women's Issues recommends that:

> **Municipalities identify housing as a priority and work with community agencies to develop housing projects (such as Habitat for Humanity) which allow women to access safe, affordable, adequate housing, with home ownership as a primary goal.**
>
> **and**
>
> **Information on housing alternatives be made widely available through community agencies and media.**
>
> **and**
>
> **Financial institutions work with government agencies to develop plans that enable women to purchase homes.**

RECOMMENDATIONS FOR THE BUSINESS COMMUNITY

Whereas:

The structure of business and the workplace has traditionally prevented the full participation of women.

Whereas:

The wage-gap remains high: married women between the ages of 45 and 65 earn just over half of what men do. Women continue to be under-represented in sciences, trades and technologies, and over-represented in lower-paying "traditional" jobs.

Whereas:

Women's employment is such that few women accumulate pension credits through long-term employment; and pension plans are income-driven which perpetuates women's low income status into retirement.

The Alberta Advisory Council on Women's Issues recommends that:

> **Business adapts its structures to the reality of women's lives, such as on-site childcare and flexible work schedules.**
>
> **and**
>
> **Business provide benefits for part-time workers.**
>
> **and**
>
> **Flexible pension plans be developed that are portable and are not income-driven.**
>
> **and**
>
> **Businesses adopt policies of employment equity in the workplace.**

RECOMMENDATIONS FOR WOMEN

Whereas:

The shift to the new knowledge economy provides a window of opportunity for women to become leaders in the new economy as they are world leaders in microenterprise, and in the development of empowering structures.

Whereas:

Knowledge is required for women to formulate strategies of abundance.

Whereas:

The economic condition of women has been minimally researched by both economists and women's studies; yet economics underlies all women's issues.

The Alberta Advisory Council on Women's Issues recommends that:

Women take the lead in forward-looking strategies in the area of childcare pooling, women's savings clubs, and researching the area of shorter work-weeks.

and

Women purposefully endeavor to increase and continually update their knowledge of economics and that they share this knowledge with women in their communities.

and

A microenterprise development bank be opened by women in Alberta.

and

Women academics and economists take a lead role in the study of women and economics.

EXECUTIVE SUMMARY

Background

The *Economic Situation of Women Over 55* was commissioned by the Alberta Advisory Council on Women's Issues. The objectives of the paper are:

1. To provide an overview of the economic situation of Alberta women over 55 at the present time.
2. To provide analysis of the projected economic situation of Alberta women who will become 55 in the next two decades.
3. To examine the effects of gender issues on women's economic status as they age to over 55 years.
4. To undertake a literature review of the economic situation of women over 55 in other developed countries, making recommendations on programs or ideas which might be suitable for Alberta.

Women Over 55

In 1991, close to 61% of Alberta women aged 55–64 had incomes which placed them under Statistics Canada Low Income Cut-off (LICO) for urban areas ($14,160). The LICO tends to understate poverty in relation to other methods of measurement. As women age it gets worse. 68% of women aged 65–74, and 71% of women over 75 have total incomes below the LICO for urban areas. In all age groups, more than three quarters of the women lived in urban areas.

The median total income of Alberta women over age 55 is $11,855. Median income is the level where one half the women have lower incomes and the other half has higher incomes. Total income is income from all sources including employment, Canada Pension Plan, Old Age Security and Guaranteed Income Supplement, and private investment income. Measures of women's total income show women's personal poverty, which is often hidden behind figures for household income.

Only 42% of women over age 65 are married, 48% are widowed. 86% of Alberta women over age 75 are widows. The majority of Alberta women over 65 do not have a spouse to share expenses with and must support themselves on the above incomes.

Causes of Women's Poor Economic Situation

The source of women's poor financial situation is structural; it is due to the way society itself is set up. There was a dominant ideology when women over 55 were in their younger years, as shown in the diagram below. Although there has been change, the same factors continue to strongly influence women's economic condition today. The factors involved are cumulative, they build upon one another and compound with interest. The following diagram shows how each factor builds upon the previous ones—and the end result.

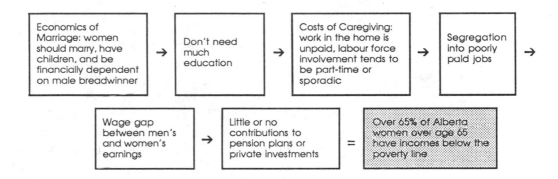

Women in the 35–54 Age Group

In the last twenty years, there has been significant social change which has improved women's economic condition. The most significant shift has been the increase in the number of women in the labour force. The following statistics will show that while there have been changes, women still have a long way to go to attain economic self-sufficiency.

Women are 49% of Alberta's population in the age group 35–54. Close to 80% live in urban areas and close to three quarters are married.

Compared to women over 55, women in the 35–54 age group:

- are better educated with close to 50% having completed high school, and 34% having some post-secondary education
- have higher average incomes, although more than two thirds of women aged 35–54 have incomes less than $25,000 annually
- have much higher labour force participation rates (80% including part-time, women are 70% of all part-time workers)

Programs

To be effective, programs must be woman-centred. The most effective programs address women's practical needs such as childcare. The factors that prevent women from being economically self-sufficient must be dealt with for a program to be successful. For example, these programs often teach women assertiveness and other lifeskills, in addition to basic business skills. Cooperative childcare programs allow the mothers to work and attend school, while learning parenting skills.

The most promising programs are those that facilitate women's microenterprise development. Traditional economic development programs usually focus on large-scale, multi-million dollar projects such as building oil processing plants or funding large corporations. Microenterprise development focuses on very small businesses at the grassroots level. Instead of millions, the amounts usually range in the hundreds or thousands. Savings clubs and microcredit lending institutions, such as the Grameen Bank of India, provide money for women to launch businesses. Other important programs reviewed were high-school apprenticeship programs, cooperative childcare, and education programs to teach women "economic literacy."

The Future

Trends that were identified included the "graying" of society, the continuing increase of women in the workforce, and the shift to the "knowledge economy". The "old" economy was based on mass-manufacturing. The knowledge economy is based on technology and information. There are both threats to women's economic well-being and opportunities for increased self-sufficiency in each of these. Some significant effects of the knowledge economy for women are:

- changes in management practices to a more empowering workplace
- the rise of microenterprise and of women business owners
- shorter work weeks
- decrease in government spending
- a shortage of skilled labour in some sectors

The economic changes being experienced globally are structural—the structure of the world's economy is changing. The old structures did not do much for women, in fact they ensured their poor financial condition—it may be for the best that they are on the way out. It is crucial that women have a strong voice in shaping what's on the way in. There is a window of opportunity for women to take the lead in the new economy. Women are world leaders in microenterprise, and in developing empowering structures. Some women are already benefitting from the new economy. Knowledge and strategy are needed to ensure opportunities in the new economy are available to all women.

Conclusions

1. A key concept is women's personal poverty. Household income is used as the measure of income in gathering statistics. Women's personal poverty is hidden in these statistics if "household income" is really the man's income. This becomes apparent when marriages end, either through divorce or death.

2. Knowledge is required for women to formulate strategies of abundance. There are plenty of opportunities in the new economy and women are well placed to take advantage of them. Women need knowledge of what changes in the economy are taking place and how to take advantage of these changes.

INTRODUCTION

The economic condition of women has been mostly ignored by both economists and Western women's studies. What stands out is the silence in each field. Economic theory is about economic *man;* women aren't even counted. Women's studies have covered many topics, but mention little of economics. This has left women with a lack of knowledge about a huge chunk of their world and how to change it.

Economics can be called "the mother of all women's issues." It underlies women's condition in society—it is the core of the rotten apple. Women will not have true choices or equality until they have economic independence.

The structure of our society has ensured that women as a group are in poor shape economically, although some areas are improving. The women's movement has brought many changes to society, and these changes are improving women's financial condition. This is clearly seen in comparing women over 55 to their younger counterparts.

We are also living in a time of incredible changes in the world's economy. These changes are structural; they are not part of a cycle. We cannot go back to the jobs, industries and the economy we once knew. The old structures certainly didn't do much for women; it may be for the best that they're on the way out. The question then becomes "What's on the way *in?*" If one is trapped in scarcity thinking (a hallmark of the "old" economics) what's *in* is doom and gloom and a lot of fear. If one is thinking abundance (a hallmark of the "new" economics) what's *in* is plenty of opportunity and lots of excitement.

Knowledge is required for women to formulate strategies of abundance. Women need knowledge of what the changes are in the economy and how to capitalize on them (to use a favourite business buzzword). This paper is a start in gaining that knowledge.

BASIC ECONOMIC THEORY

This section will give the basic assumptions, beliefs and definitions of economic theory shared by all major schools of economic thought. A full analysis of the impact of economic theory is beyond the scope of this paper; the intent is to show that the factors affecting women's economic conditions are no accident—they stem directly from the beliefs surrounding economics.

Commonly Used Economic Terms *(found in italics)*

The most common definition of economics is "the study of the use of scarce resources to satisfy unlimited human wants" (Lipsey et al, 1991). Economic theory is based on the assumption of scarcity—that there is not enough and that humans are innately greedy. *Resources* include natural resources such as trees, land, and minerals; human resources, both mental and physical; and manufactured aids to production such as tools, machinery and buildings. These resources are called *factors of production* because they are used to produce those things that people want. The things produced are called *commodities*, which is divided into *goods* and *services*. Goods are tangible (cars, shoes) and services are intangible (education, haircut). The act of making goods and services is called *production* and the act of using them is called *consumption* (Lipsey et al, 1991). Consumption refers to spending, not to eating or wearing out old clothes (Waring, 1992). People *exchange* one asset for another to satisfy needs, only those exchanges that involve paying *money* are called consumption.

"Modern" economics is based on the work of Adam Smith who wrote "The Wealth of Nations" in 1776. In that book he laid out the foundations of economics which are still used today. They are: the importance of *freedom of trade* (allowing goods to move freely i.e. without duties and tariffs between countries) and the *division of labour* (which means breaking up a task into a number of smaller, *specialized* tasks so each worker can become more skilled and faster at their job, i.e. an assembly line); the dangers of government protection of monopolies (where a product or service is controlled by one company), and the imposition of tariffs or duties; and the superiority of self-interest over altruism as a means of improving the economy's efficiency (Baumol et al, 1988). A free market system, in other words. A *free market system* is defined as an economy organized so that decisions on resource allocation are left to the independent decisions of individual producers and consumers acting in their own best interest

> "Each great era of growth in history has been based not on scarcity at all, but on *abundance*. Economic expansions have been based on readily available, cheap steel; then cheap energy, particularly oil; and now with vast supplies of cheap microchips. This flies in the face of everything we've ever been taught about economics."
>
> Nuala Beck, economist

without central direction. *Supply and demand* determine *prices*. Those workers with valuable skills and owners of scarce resources will be able to sell what they have at high prices. With the incomes they earn they can then purchase the goods and services they want most, within the limits of their budget. "Those with less to sell will have to live more frugally" (Baumol, 1988).

An *economic system* determines what to produce, how to produce it and who gets it. There are three main economic schools of thought, all of them based on Adam's assumptions of human behavior: free market, mixed and centrally planned. These systems can be placed on a continuum. On the right is Smith's *"laissez-faire"* (leave it alone) market system. This has also been called *neo-classical* or *pure capitalism*. On the left is the centrally planned economy where the government controls the bulk of economic decision making. The mainstream of economics is the mixed economy, which has a mix of market determination and government intervention (which usually centres around attempting to ensure an adequate living standard for all people). The mix varies from country to country and province to province.

Economic Theory and Women

Economic theory is based on assumptions, whether implicit or explicit. Economists admit that their work is based on assumptions to the extent that a favorite joke (about a chemist, a physicist and an economist being stranded on a desert isle with ample canned food, but no opener—the economist's solution is "Let's assume a can opener") appears in most economics texts and books. Economists tend to view their simplifications as relatively innocent. We shall see that, especially for women, they're not.

The explicit assumption that people are selfish in markets [because of scarcity, that there is "not enough"] is generally accepted by economists (Frank, 1988). "Smith noted that people were very good at pursuing their own self-interest, and that a market system was a very good way to harness this self-interest. As he put it, with clear religious overtones, in doing what is best for themselves, people are 'led by an invisible hand' to promote the economic well-being of society" (Baumol et al, 1988). The "people" Smith was referring to were men; he believed women belonged at home.

"Our current economic teachings assume as unquestionable that 'the economic man' will never do anything unless he has to; will only do it to escape pain or attain pleasure; and will, inevitably, take all he can get and do all he can to outwit, overcome, and if necessary, destroy his antagonist."

Charlotte Perkins Gilman, suffragette

"Work is still the primary means by which people establish a claim to a share of production. To be without work is to place that claim in jeopardy" (Newland, 1979). Work, labour and economic activity are often used interchangeably by economists. They mean those activities that produce surplus value, i.e. profits in the marketplace. Any activity that does not directly produce profits is not work. This is how the United Nations, and every country in the world, defines work.

"Thus the international economic system constructs reality in a way that excludes the great bulk of women's work— reproduction (in all its forms), raising children, domestic work, and subsistence production. Cooking, according to economists, is 'active labour' when cooked food is sold and 'economically inactive labour' when it is not. Housework is 'productive' when performed by a paid domestic servant and 'nonproductive' when no payment is involved. Those who care for children in an orphanage are 'occupied'; mothers who care for their children at home are 'unoccupied' " (Waring, 1988).

How Women's Work Isn't Counted

These assumptions and definitions comprise the thinking behind the United Nations System of National Accounts (UNSNA). UNSNA is the system used globally to measure and record the economic activity of a country. National accounts were originally developed to measure the income of a country at war (both the United States and Britain during World War II). The system was designed to justify the huge war expenditures which outstripped the national income. A system was needed to balance the books of a country at war. It was not designed to measure the well-being of a country's population.

The national accounts are used to determine a country's income or Gross Domestic Product (GDP). GDP is the sum of the money values of all final goods and services produced by the economy within a certain time period, usually one year— whether the resources used are owned by the country's residents or not (Gross National Product or GNP is the same thing but only counts those factors of production owned by a country's people). Anything outside the *production boundary* is not counted in the GDP—including all of women's unpaid work, household maintenance and production (i.e. a garden), and illegal activities.

"Reasons given by men for their failure to account for women's work are 1) conceptual problems, and 2) the practical difficulties of collecting data. It does not seem to occur to them that if you have a conceptual problem about the activity of half the human species, you then have a conceptual problem about the whole."

Marilyn Waring, economist

"When it dawns on you that militarism and the destruction of the environment are recorded as growth, it is the UNSNA that has made it so. When you yearn for a breath of nature's fresh air or a glass of radio-active free water, remember that the UNSNA says that both are worthless."

Marilyn Waring

"If we recognized home-making and child rearing as productive work to be included in the national economic accounts, the receipt of welfare might not imply dependency. But we don't. It may be hoped the women's movement of the present time will change that. But at the time I write, it has not."

Daniel Moynihan, U.S. Senator

Both the GDP and GNP are used to monitor rates and patterns of growth, to set priorities in policy making, to measure the success of policies, and to measure "economic welfare." Since the bulk of women's work is left out of the GDP, it is not a large step to leaving them out of policy considerations altogether (Waring, 1988). Some current examples are the "welfare mom" who doesn't "work" and the national debt. The figures often quoted for the debt compares the debt to GDP. If women's work was counted, Canada's GDP would increase by 25–30% (United Nations, 1991) and our current debt position would look much better.

How Women Are Further Left Out

In economics, consumers and persons aren't counted—households are. A household, in economic terms, is all the people who live under one roof and who make joint financial decisions or are subject to others making such decisions for them (Lipsey, 1991). Economists make several assumptions about households: 1) that each household makes consistent decisions, as though it were composed of a single individual, 2) households are the principal owners of factors of production (human beings), whose services they sell to firms and receive incomes in return, and 3) each household seeks maximum satisfaction or utility within the limitations of its resources.

"Despite the boasts of flexibility in the household survey system, the well-being of a population will never be truly assessed while households remain the respondent unit."

Marilyn Waring

These assumptions hide women; they're not individuals but part of a household. This is responsible for some damaging policies such as the "man in the house" rule for social support programs, where as soon as a woman moves in with a man she loses her benefits; and war veteran's widows being cut off from their dead husbands' pensions when they remarry. This system also hides information about a woman's individual situation in a household because the "head" of the household answers the questions on the Census form. Household income masks women's personal poverty, if the "household" income is really the man's. This is an important concept—women's personal poverty means that many women are "one man away from poverty."

A more implicit assumption in this area is that men behave selfishly in the market but altruistically at home. As the typical "head" of the family was, and is, male with a wife and children dependent upon him for providing for their needs, it is assumed that he will behave rationally and seek satisfaction for all family members. The recent Statistics Canada (1993) survey on family violence casts doubt on this altruistic behavior (29% of all women who have been married or have lived in a common-law relationship have experienced criminal code violence from their partner). "By subsuming the needs of all family members into one utility function, the story of the benevolent patriarch provides an economic parallel to the historical invisibility of children and women in much of British and American law" (Strassmann, 1993).

The second assumption is that the "household" (i.e. the male breadwinner) sells its services in return for an income. Women who work in the home are not paid, cannot contribute to pensions, and end up poor as a result.

The household and the thinking behind it serves as a background to theories of income distribution, taxation, welfare, and economic development (Strassmann, 1993). Canada's tax system is based on the marital unit and assumes that income is shared equally within the family. It also makes it more difficult for a woman to work outside the home because the family may lose the varied credits that are based on family income. In divorce, child support payments are taxed as income for the person receiving them [usually the mother], while they are a deduction for the person paying [usually the father] (Canadian Advisory Council on the Status of Women, 1993).

"I finally got child support six years after our divorce. By then all it did was punish me by raising my tax bracket."

Lauren

THE CURRENT SITUATION OF WOMEN OVER 55

DEMOGRAPHIC INFORMATION

Any differences in data totals are due to rounding of the data—Statistics Canada rounds to the nearest five or zero.

The quotes in this section are from the women interviewed for this paper. Their profiles are at the back of the paper, pages 69–70.

Number and Percentage of Women by Age Groups

In 1991, there were 223,735 women over 55 in Alberta which is 9% of the entire Alberta population and 18% of the female population of Alberta. The percentage of women in each age group increases with age due to the longer life expectancy of women, as the following chart illustrates.

Age Group	% of Women in Age Group	Number
55 - 59	49	48,520
60 - 64	50	44,995
65 - 69	53	41,075
70 - 74	55	32,965
75 - 79	58	25,580
80 - 84	61	16,650
85 - 89	63	9,085
90 and over	69	4,865
Total		223,735

Source: Statistics Canada. Age, Sex and Marital Status. Ottawa: Supply and Services Canada, 1992. 1991 Census of Canada. Catalogue No. 93-310.

Life Expectancy

Women live longer than men do, which means their retirement savings must stretch out over more years. In 1991, women aged 65 in Alberta can expect to live 20.33 more years, women aged 80 may live another 9.91 years and women aged 85 have, on average, 7.29 years of life left (Alberta Bureau of Statistics, 1993).

Location

The great majority of women over 55 live in urban areas. The number of women living on farms decreases with age. This may reflect a move to gain access to services available in the larger cities or to nursing homes or lodges, or be a result of no longer being able to afford to keep the farm. Rural women tend to experience fewer job opportunities, limited housing and childcare options and less available social services than their urban counterparts.

Age Group	Urban Areas	Rural Farm	Rural non-farm
55-59	78%	9%	13%
60-64	79%	8%	13%
65-74	81%	5%	14%
Over 75	86%	2%	13%
Total	81%	6%	13%

Source: Statistics Canada. Profile of Urban and Rural Areas, Part A, Canada, Provinces and Territories. Ottawa: Industry, Science and Technology Canada, 1993. 1991 Census of Canada. Catalogue No. 93-339.

Ethnic Origin

Women in Alberta come from a mix of ethnic origins. The percentages in the following table do not add up to 100% since Statistics Canada allows census respondents to list more than one ethnic origin. This allows a more complete picture of the ethnic origins of Canadians. Statistics Canada designates responses either as single origin (i.e. Ukrainian) or as multiple origin
(i.e. French-Canadian).

Age Group	Canadian	British	French	European	Asian
45-64	3.89%	63.31%	8.73%	52.43%	6.00%
Over 65	2.25%	55.89%	5.43%	41.74%	4.57%

Age Group	Arab	Latin, Central, South American	Caribbean	Inuit	Metis	North American Indian
45-64	0.35%	0.15%	0.19%	0.04%	1.17%	2.02%
Over 65	0.17%	0.08%	0.05%	0.02%	0.60%	0.85%

Source: Statistics Canada. Ethnic Origin. Ottawa: Supply and Services Canada, 1992. 1991 Census of Canada. Catalogue No. 93-315.

"Immigrating was traumatic for me. It was starting all over again at 50, to prove what I have. You feel like a stranger, a one-dimensional person. I felt very grateful for being accepted into Canada, and I wanted to do something for this country."

Diana

Both Native and immigrant women are over-represented among the working poor. Women of visible minorities face racial discrimination and immigrant women may have language barriers to education and employment. Professional immigrant women often cannot gain accreditation in Canada and cannot work in their area of specialty. Immigrant women are ghettoized in poorly paid sectors where they work as domestics, chambermaids, waitresses, dishwashers, sewing machine operators and building cleaners (Edmonton Immigrant Women, 1990). Elderly women who have recently immigrated may not be eligible for old age benefits that are based on residency requirements.

Marital Status

> "Things are not made easy for women if they don't have a husband. If you don't have a man behind you, you are blocked in many ways."
>
> Diana

Women over 55 in Alberta are likely to be married or widowed, and after the age of 65, the majority of women are widows. 86% of women over the age of 75 are widowed. Senior women are more likely to be widowed than men because they typically are younger than their husbands and they have a longer life expectancy. The divorce rate for women has increased following legislated reforms in 1968. The number of lesbians or their relationship status is unknown.

Age Group	Single	Married	Separated	Widowed	Divorced
55-59	4%	74%	3%	10%	10%
60-64	4%	69%	2%	17%	8%
Over 65	5%	42%	2%	48%	4%

Source: Statistics Canada. Age, Sex and Marital Status. Ottawa: Supply and Services Canada, 1992. 1991 Census of Canada. Catalogue No. 93-310.

The following chart shows the decline in married status and the rise in widowhood as the age of the women increases:

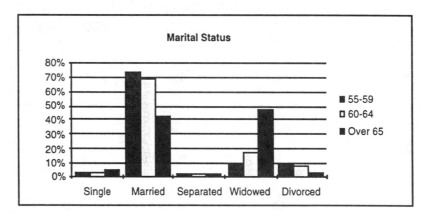

Common-law relationships are not common among women over 55. Few women over 55 live in common-law relationships. The following table is an illustration of the marital status of women living in common-law relationships. For example, a woman may have been previously married and divorced, and is now living in a common-law relationship.

Age Group	Single	Separated	Widowed	Divorced	Total
55-59	0%	0%	0%	1%	2%
60-64	0%	0%	0%	1%	1%
65 and over	0%	0%	0%	0%	1%

Source: Statistics Canada. Age, Sex and Marital Status. Ottawa: Supply and Services Canada, 1992. 1991 Census of Canada. Catalogue No. 93-310.

Number of Children

Fertility is measured by Statistics Canada as the number of children ever born alive to women over the age of 15. 1991 was the first time the question regarding number of children was asked to all women over age 15. In previous years, it was only asked to ever-married women.

The women over 55 were the mothers of the "baby boom" (commonly defined as the years between 1945—1964). The fertility rate for these women was higher than in succeeding years as reflected in the percentage of women who had three or more children, and the relatively high percentage of women who had more than six children.

Age Group	None	1	2	3	4	5	6+
55 - 59	9%	7%	20%	24%	17%	10%	13%
60 - 64	9%	8%	20%	21%	16%	11%	16%
65 - 69	11%	9%	21%	20%	15%	10%	14%
Over 70	13%	12%	22%	18%	13%	8%	14%

Statistics Canada. Fertility. Ottawa: Supply and Services Canada, 1992. 1991 Census of Canada. Catalogue No. 93-321.

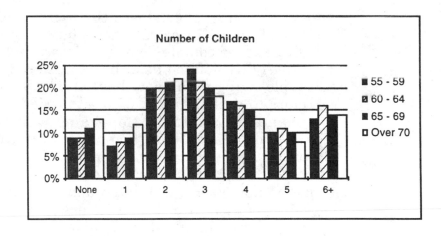

Living Arrangements—Private Households

Most Alberta women lived in private households in 1991. A private household is any living arrangement that is not an institutional setting. As women age, they are more likely to live alone when they become widowed. Only 2% of women aged 55–64 lived with related family, this increased to 7% of women over 75.

The number of lone female parents for the age group 55–64 was 5,660 or 6% of the total age group. There were 430 (.4%) lone female parents over the age of 65 (Statistics Canada, 1992). Women who are lone parents in the 55–64 age group enter the "empty nest" stage of life. Once their children leave home, child support, family allowance payments, and in many cases, eligibility for subsidized housing cease. Low-income parents often cannot afford to help finance their children's education. This increases the risk that their children will also be low-income .

185 women lived with their unmarried children. There were 360 women over 55 living with their parents. These women may have the task of caring for their very elderly parents while their own health may be deteriorating.

The following table shows the living arrangements for women over 55 living in private households. Statistics Canada has some rather complex ways of describing this information. *"Family"* is defined as either a husband-wife or common-law couple living with or without children. *"With related family"* refers to women living with a married or common-law couple who are related to her (for example, living with her daughter and son in-law). *"With non-related family"* refers to women living with a married or common-law couple, in which neither person is related to her (for example, a woman who is boarding in the home of an unrelated married couple). Women living *"with relative"* are those who are living with any relative other than a family (for example, a sister or niece who are neither married or living common-law). Women living *"with non-relative"* are those living with anyone who is neither married or living common-law, and who is not related to her (a friend, for example).

"We were conditioned to be wife and mother, to be in the home all our lives. We were never told what to do if we left, how to be a single mom. I had to figure it out as I went along."

Joan

Age Group	With Spouse, common-law partner or lone parent	With Parent(s)	With Related Family	With Non-related Family	With Relative	With Non Relative	Alone
55-64	72,400	265	2,090	235	1,545	1,530	13,980
65-74	42,980	65	2,860	120	1,930	1,145	22,490
Over 75	14,115	15	3,160	100	2,155	750	23,640

Source: Statistics Canada. Families: Number, Type and Structure. Ottawa: Supply and Services Canada, 1992. 1991 Census of Canada. Catalogue 93-312.

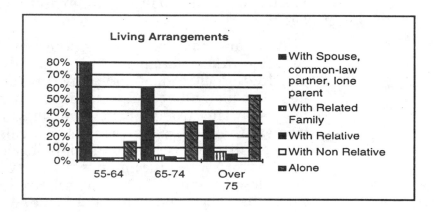

Renting vs. Owning

The following chart shows the number of female primary maintainers who own their homes. A primary maintainer is the person who pays most of the shelter expenses. In the case where people share these expenses equally, the first person listed on the census form is chosen. When compared to the total number of women living in private households (whether or not they are primary maintainers) it shows that few women own their homes. It is unknown if the houses are mortgage-free, however most people have finished their mortgage payments by the age of 65. The number of women who co-own houses with their spouse or another person is unknown from the available data.

Age Group	# of Female Primary Maintainers who Own	% of Women Living in Private Households who are Primary Maintainers
55-64	16,975	18%
65-74	19,690	28%
Over 75	15,805	36%

Source: Statistics Canada. Dwellings and Households. Ottawa: Supply and Services Canada, 1992. 1991 Census of Canada. Catalogue No. 93-311.

We rented this house for 24 years. I wanted to buy it but my husband didn't want to. Now I have to pay the rent on my own."

Karen

Owning your own home is one of the best ways to build equity and protect yourself from inflation (as years go by, mortgage payments tend to decrease while rents increase). Unfortunately many women have not had the opportunity to take advantage of this fact.

Senior homeowners may experience affordability problems if their income is not sufficient to meet the cash expenses necessary to maintain their homes. If they are forced to sell, rent payments and inflation will eventually erode their equity and leave them with no assets or cash reserves. This is a reality for women as they can expect to live 20 years past the age of 65.

Widows are most likely to own their own home which is reflected in more women owning as they get older. The distribution of income and property from divorce settlements has kept many divorced women from owning a home. While never-married women have higher incomes than all other women, their average income is still relatively low and may not permit the purchase of a home. It can be very difficult for a woman with a low income to save $8-12,000 (plus legal fees) for a down-payment (10% was required when these women would have been purchasing a home).

Women Living in Collective Dwellings

Collective dwellings are commercial, institutional, or communal in nature. This category includes chronic care hospitals, nursing homes, senior citizen residences and hospitals. There has been a decline in seniors living in collective dwellings since 1971. In 1971, 13.3% of all seniors lived in collective dwellings compared to 9% in 1991. The percentage of seniors living alone also increased during this time from 21.4% in 1971 to 27% in 1991. These changes may be due to the development of the Home Care/Community Long Term Care Program, the building of subsidized housing for seniors, or the increase in income support for older persons during these years (Seniors Advisory Council for Alberta, 1993).

However, 21% of all women over age 75 lived in collective dwellings in 1991. The reasons a woman may be institutionalized range from failing health, a disability, little or no income to support herself, lack of home care services (especially in rural areas), or no outside social or economic support to enable her to continue to live at home or with others.

Age Group	Corrections Institution	Hospital	Special Care Homes	Other	Total
55-64	0	150	400	420	970
65-74	0	245	1,440	355	2,040
Over 75	0	800	10,790	325	11,915

Note:
Hospital: more than a six-month stay in either general or psychiatric hospital
Special Care Home: includes nursing care homes, lodges, extended care centres
Other: includes religious orders, Hutterite colonies, rooming houses and hotels

Source: Statistics Canada. Dwellings and Households. Ottawa: Supply and Services Canada, 1992. 1991 Census of Canada. Catalogue No. 93-311.

The following chart shows the distribution of the collective settings women lived in. 71% of women over 65 and 91% of women over 75 lived in special care homes. There were no older women living in correctional institutions.

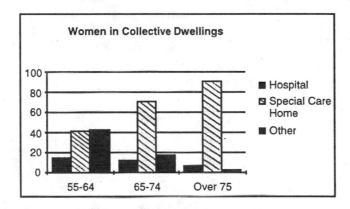

Women With Disabilities

The following table includes women with mobility, agility, seeing, hearing, speaking and unknown disabilities who live in private households. The remaining number of women with disabilities live in a collective dwelling. As women age, they are more likely to become disabled. Almost one-quarter of women aged 55–64 have a disability. As this group is not yet eligible for pension benefits, their disability could create financial hardship if it keeps them from working, especially if they have no other financial support.

Age Group	With Disability	Total in Age Group	% With Disability
55-64	21,770	93,515	23%
65-74	20,340	74,040	27%
75-84	15,450	42,230	37%
Over 85	2,685	13,950	19%

Source: Statistics Canada. Subprovincial Data for Alberta. Ottawa: Supply and Services Canada, 1989. 1987 HALS Survey. Catalogue No. 82-611.

Education Levels

As a group, older women are not well educated. More than 62% of the women over age 75 and 51% of women aged 65–74 did not complete high school. Women who were never married and divorced women tend to have higher levels of education. The lack of education makes it difficult for married women to support themselves if it becomes necessary, as in the case of divorce or early widowhood. Lack of education forces many women to take unskilled jobs with low pay. Many low-paying service jobs require long hours of standing, which may be difficult for older women.

> "Going back to school was the hardest thing I ever did. I went to class all day, got home to cook dinner and be with the kids, and would be up 'til 3 a.m. doing my own homework. It was hard to concentrate in class if one of the kids had a problem."
>
> Joan

Age Group	None	1-4 yrs	5-8 yrs	9-10 yrs	11-13 yrs	14-17 yrs	18+ yrs
55 - 64	2%	2%	15%	22%	39%	16%	3%
65 - 74	2%	3%	23%	23%	36%	12%	1%
Over 75	4%	7%	30%	21%	27%	10%	1%

Source: Statistics Canada. Educational Attainment and School Attendance. Ottawa: Supply and Services Canada, 1992. 1991 Census of Canada. Catalogue No. 93-328.

> "Now I wish I had education more than I ever have."
>
> Karen

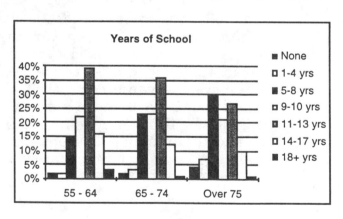

ECONOMIC INFORMATION

An important concept in this section is the measure of poverty. The Statistics Canada Low Income Cut-off (LICO) is one such measure. The LICO assumes that a family or individual spends an excessive proportion of its income on the basic necessities such as food, clothing and shelter. The LICO is set at the point where families, on average, spend more than 20% of their income than did the average family on these necessities. The LICO is adjusted to account for differences in family size and location (urban or rural) (Spector, 1992). The Statistics Canada estimates are conservative when compared to other poverty measures, it is quite likely that the incidence of poverty for unattached elderly women is underestimated. The 1990 LICO was $14,160 for an individual and $28,090 for a family of four living in cities of over 500,000 (Edmonton and Calgary); and $9,640 for an individual living in a rural area.

Income as a measure does not account for owning assets such as a mortgage-free house or loan-free car. Having no mortgage or rent payments can allow women who own their homes to have a comfortable lifestyle on a lower income. Measures of women's individual income is where their personal poverty becomes obvious. Women living with their spouse may be quite comfortable due to sharing his income; they may not feel poor. Yet the majority of Alberta women over 55 do not have sufficient personal incomes to support themselves if necessary.

Total Income

Women over 55 in Alberta are, as a group, income poor and it gets worse with age. Close to 61% of women aged 55–64 are under the LICO for urban areas, this rises to 68% for women aged 65–74 and 71% for women over age 75. As was noted previously, most older women live in urban areas.

The following table and chart show the distribution of women's total income in constant 1990 dollars. Constant dollars are adjusted for inflation so comparisons can be made between different years.

Age Group	None	Under $9,999	$10,000-14,999	$15,000-24,999	$25,000-39,999	Over $40,000
55 - 64	13%	35%	13%	18%	13%	7%
65 - 69	3%	37%	28%	18%	10%	5%
Over 70	1%	22%	48%	16%	8%	5%

Source: Statistics Canada. Selected Income Statistics. Ottawa: Supply and Services Canada, 1992. 1991 Census of Canada. Catalogue No. 93-331.

"My husband went away on business trips and would leave me with no money. My neighbour gave us soup bones and the kids and I would eat soup for the week."

Karen

"I don't know how you can do it without men thinking you're selfish, but insist on a joint bank account and a certain amount of money of your own."

Karen

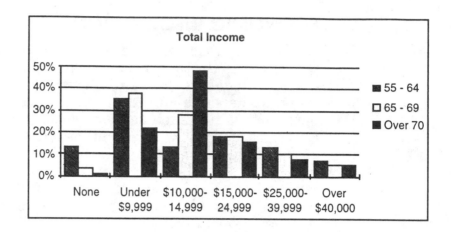

Average Total Income

The average and median total incomes for each age group are shown in the following table. The median income is the level where one half of the women in each category have higher incomes and one half have lower incomes. It is obvious that many women are well below the Low Income Cut- off. One half of women aged 55–64 have incomes 9% below the LICO for an urban individual, one half of women aged 65–69 have incomes 21% below the LICO and one-half of women over 75 have incomes 19% below the LICO.

Age	Average Incomes		Median Incomes	
	1985	1990	1985	1990
55 - 64	$16,953	$17,417	$12,239	$12,830
65 - 69	$14,643	$15,666	$10,917	$11,249
70 and over	$14,379	$15,824	$10,997	$11,485

Source: Statistics Canada. Selected Income Statistics. Ottawa: Industry, Science and Technology Canada, 1993. 1991 Census of Canada. Catalogue # 93-331.

Full-year, Full-time Employment Income and Marital Status

The following table shows average full-year, full-time employment income (defined by Statistics Canada as more than 30 hours a week for 49 to 52 weeks of the year). In the 55–64 age group, single (never-married) women earned the highest average income with divorced women second highest and married women lowest. This could be due to education levels as never-married and divorced women tend to have higher levels of education. Nationally, women who were separated, divorced or widowed made about $3,000 a year more than their married or single counterparts.

> "Women in their fifties are not accepted as good employees."
>
> Diana

Age Group	Single	Married	Separated	Widowed	Divorced	Average
55 - 64	$29,947	$22,141	$23,580	$23,788	$25,943	$23,251
Over 65	$15,484	$16,990	XXX	$18,330	$25,395	$18,065

Source: Statistics Canada. Selected Income Statistics. Ottawa: Industry, Science and Technology Canada, 1993. 1991 Census of Canada. Catalogue # 93-331.

Never-married women drop almost $15,000 in average employment income when they reach the over 65 age group. It may be that the women in this group who had higher paying jobs retired, while their lower paid cohorts continued to work. Married and widowed women also dropped in average earnings when they enter this age group, probably for the same reason. There is no data on separated women for the over 65 age group, since only 1% of women over 65 are separated.

Private Pension and RRSP Income

Information on employer sponsored pension plan, RRSP (Registered Retirement Savings Plan) and investment income was not available for Alberta women. The following information is based on statistics for all Canadian women.

> "I only started saving after the kids were grown and moved away from home. Before that it was tough to even make ends meet."
>
> Joan

In 1979, only 6% of all women aged 18 to 70 participated in RRSPs. This had increased to 19% by 1989. By 1989, women accounted for 41% of all contributors to RRSP plans. 91% of the money contributed to women's RRSPs was contributed by themselves, while the balance came from husbands in the form of spousal contributions. The growth in the number of women with RRSPs is due to their increased participation in the work force (Frenken, 1991). RRSP participation is weaker in the 55–64 age group, either because of limited income at their disposal or because they have already retired and prefer to put their money to other uses (Galarneau, 1991). In 1988, 25% of women aged 45–54 contributed to an RRSP.

42% of working women are in employer-sponsored pension plans compared to 54% of men. Women's lower rates are because they account for a higher proportion of part-time workers (70%). They are also over-represented in sectors such as business and personal services where coverage rates are lower. In 1989, 35% of women aged 55 and over had pension coverage, while just under 50% of women aged 35–54 were covered (Frenken and Maser, 1992).

In 1990, more than half of all taxpayers reported interest and dividend income accounting for 13% of their total income. Although nearly equal numbers of men and women reported investment income, the composition of this income was quite different. Of dividend recipients, 43% were women and they received 35% of all dividends reported. Dividends made up 12% of their investment income. Since investment income is directly related to total income, women would be expected to have less investment income than men. However, in 1990, women's aggregate investment income ($19.3 billion) was only marginally below that of men ($19.8 billion). This can be explained by women's longevity. Since wives generally outlive their husbands, the inheritance of their spouse's financial assets, in addition to their own, results in an increased level of investment income. This income, which was formerly split between them, is now claimed only by the wife (Siroonian, 1993). In 1990, 45% of taxfilers reporting investment income aged 75 and over were unattached women.

Labour Force Participation Rates

The labour force participation rate for Alberta women has increased overall since 1971. The labour force is comprised of people working either full or part-time and those unemployed looking for work. The labour force participation rate is the labour force divided by the total population. Women in the labour force contribute to Canada Pension Plans and perhaps private pension plans, and earn an income which may allow them to save for retirement. The following table shows women's labour force participation rates since 1971:

Age Group	1971	1976	1981	1986	1991
55 - 59	44.5	47	48.6	52.8	58.9
60 - 64	32.4	33	32.2	33.1	36.2
65 and over	8.0	8.5	6.6	5.1	7.2

Source: Statistics Canada. Labour Force Activity. Ottawa: Industry, Science and Technology Canada, 1993. 1991 Census of Canada. Catalogue # 93-324.

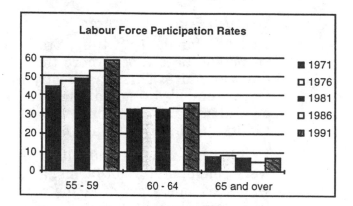

The labour force participation rates drop significantly for the over 65 group which indicates many women probably retire at this age. Women who develop disabilities as they age, or whose disabilities progress to where they cannot work, may also be reflected in this change. Women with disabilities are half as likely to participate in the labour force as non-disabled women; this worsens with age.

In 1991, over one-half of women aged 55–59 were in the labour force and one-third of women aged 60-64 remained in the labour force.

Much of women's paid labour force work is part-time. In 1991, 36% of Canadian women employed part-time reported they did not want a full-time job, while another 22% were attending school. However, 27% of women part-time workers wanted to work full-time but could not find a full-time job. Another 13% worked part-time because of personal or family responsibilities (24% of women aged 25–44). Older women (65% of those aged 45–64) are more likely to work part-time because they did not want to work full-time (Ghalam, 1993).

Self-employment

7.4% of Alberta women were self-employed in 1991. Their ages are unknown. Of these, 2.8% had paid help. Women own and operate nearly one third of all small businesses in Canada. The number of self-employed women increased by 265% over the last two decades (compared to 74% for men). Reasons for becoming self-employed range from being laid off, wanting more freedom or wanting to have more time for family.

Women Farm Operators

In 1991, for the first time, Statistics Canada allowed Census respondents to report more than one farm operator on the questionnaire. This was mostly in response to requests from farm women's organizations. The fact that many women co-own farms and contribute to their operation was formerly hidden behind the "head" of household reporting ownership.

In 1991, there were 800 Albertan women over age 55 who were sole operators of farms, and 4,880 women over age 55 who were operators of farms with two or more operators. Women make up 22% of all farm operators in the over 55 age group (Statistics Canada, Agricultural Profile of Alberta, 1993).

Nationally, one quarter of farm operators were women. Of the women who operated farms, 37% (7,795) also had some off-farm days of work in 1991 (Statistics Canada, 1992).

PROGRAMS FOR ALBERTA WOMEN OVER 55

Federal Government Income Support Programs

Old Age Security and Guaranteed Income Supplement
The Old Age Security (OAS) program is the first tier of Canada's three-tiered retirement income system. The Canada Pension Plan and the Quebec Pension Plan make up the second tier and private pensions, investments and savings make up the third.

Old Age Security is a monthly benefit available to people age 65 or over who meet the Canadian residence and legal residence requirements. Previous employment is not a factor in determining eligibility, nor is it necessary to be retired.

The Guaranteed Income Supplement (GIS) is an income-tested, monthly benefit for Old Age Security pensioners with limited income apart from the Old Age Security pension. The amount of the supplement is based on marital status, income and the amount of Old Age Security pension being received. OAS and the GIS are adjusted quarterly to reflect increases in the cost of living as measured by the Consumer Price Index.

As of July 1, 1994, the OAS, GIS, and GST Tax Credit will total an estimated maximum of $10,432 for single seniors and $16,918 for two-senior couples and one-senior couples in which the non-senior spouse is receiving Spouse's Allowance (Alberta Community Development, 1994).

Canada Pension Plan

The Canada Pension Plan is a basic pension equal to 25% of the contributor's average monthly pensionable earnings. The maximum monthly benefit payable in 1988 was $543.06. Eligibility requirements are that contributions must have been credited to the plan in at least one year and the person claiming must be at least 65, or 60 to 64 and have wholly or substantially ceased working. Between the ages of 60 to 64, the basic pension is reduced by .5% for each month between the date the pension begins and the month after the applicant's 65th birthday; between the ages of 65 to 70, it is increased by .5%; and after age 70 it is increased by 30%.

The CPP has a surviving spouse's pension which provides for payment of survivor benefits to the legal or common–law spouse. There is also a disability pension for people under age 65 who have contributed to the plan and who have a severe and prolonged disability. Payments for both these pensions are based on income and benefit credits.

The average annual CPP benefit for Canadian women in 1989 was $3,120. This produced a total income of $10,204 when combined with Old Age Security and GIS. The poverty line for 1989 was $12,037 for most Canadian cities.

Spouse's Allowance and Widowed Spouse's Allowance

The Spouse's Allowance is for spouses age 60–64 of low-income pensioners. This benefit is also payable to low-income widows and widowers aged 60–64 irrespective of the spouse's age at death and is then called the Widowed Spouse's Allowance. In December, 1992 there were 7,108 Alberta women receiving this benefit.

Provincial Government Income Support Programs

Alberta Seniors Benefit

The Alberta Seniors Benefit is an income tested program which provides income supplement and shelter support. It will replace four current seniors benefits programs (Alberta Assured Income Plan, Property Tax Reduction Program, Senior Citizens' Renter Assistance Program, Health Care Insurance Waiver) on July 1, 1994. Benefits are based on three factors: income (with OAS and GIS as a base), marital status, and accommodation.

Maximum benefits are received by seniors who are eligible for OAS and whose income is equal to the base income from federal sources (OAS, GIS, and GST Tax Credit). Benefits are reduced for each dollar of income earned according to a sliding scale. The maximum annual cash benefit for a single senior homeowner is $1,800, which when added to federal amounts equals an annual income of $12,232. For a single senior renter, the respective amounts are $2,350 and $12,782. Two-senior couples who own their home receive a maximum of $2,950 for a total of $19,868, and two-senior couples who rent receive $3,500 for a maximum annual total of $20,418 (Alberta Community Development, 1994).

The income threshold, which is the point at which cash benefits cease, are $18,000 for single seniors, $23,000 for one-senior couples, and $27,000 for two-senior couples. Health care premiums are phased in at fifteen cents for every dollar of private income earned above these thresholds. Seniors will pay full health care insurance premiums at $20,560 for single seniors, $28,120 for one-senior couples, and $32,120 for two-senior couples (Alberta Community Development, 1994).

Alberta Widow's Pension Program (Alberta Family and Social Services)

This benefit is available to widowed men or women aged 55 to 64 with little or no income. In 1992/93, there were 3,092 recipients. This benefit is based on income level.

Alberta Supports for Independence and Alberta Assured Income for the Severely Handicapped (AISH) (Alberta Family and Social Services)

The Alberta Supports for Independence is a social allowance program based on income, assets and need which may apply to several groups of seniors. There are a small number of seniors, such as recent immigrants, who are not eligible for the federal and provincial income support programs for persons over age 65. There are also seniors with large dependent families. In June 1992, 848 women over 65 were recipients, 623 in the age group 65–74, 195 aged 75–84 and 30 who were over age 80.

AISH benefits are dependent on the income and physical/mental status of the recipient. As of June 1992, there were 102 women over 65 receiving AISH, 84 aged 65–74, 17 aged 75–84 and 1 woman over 85 (Seniors Advisory Council of Alberta, 1992).

FACTORS AFFECTING WOMEN'S ECONOMIC SITUATION

While we do know about the current economic condition of women over 55, we don't know much about their work histories. For example, the 1984 Statistics Canada Family History Survey contains information on the work history of men and women but no one over the age of 65 was interviewed. "We simply do not know much about the characteristics of female employment from a longitudinal perspective" (Gee and Kimball, 1987). Women simply weren't studied much in the 1950's and 60's; or in the 1980's, it seems!

The current economic situation of women over 55 can be understood by looking at the larger factors in play during these women's younger years. These women's lives must be understood in the context of the dominant social forces of their younger years.

The Economics of Marriage

The social ideal when these women were younger was that a woman's place was in the home caring for husband and children for no pay (as long as the family could afford it). This norm has been called "domestic ideology" (Olson, 1990) and slavery (Waring, 1988). Whatever it is called, it is clear from the previous section that the economic rewards for adhering to it are poor indeed. The domestic ideology has as its rules that 1) women should marry, 2) women should bear and raise children, and   3) women should be economically dependent on a male breadwinner (Olson, 1990). Although all three rules contribute to women's later life conditions, the third rule in particular is the source of these women's financial difficulties later in life.

Many women live on the margins of poverty throughout their lives. Because most women marry, their *personal* poverty is masked behind measures of household income (Tindale et al, 1983). While the average income in 1991 for husband-wife families in Alberta was $55,825, this does not mean that the wife is earning half of this sum. **It is when marriages end, either through divorce or death, that women's personal poverty becomes apparent.** Poverty for women is heavily concentrated among those who are widowed, divorced and separated (Morgan, 1991). Arendell (1987) found that women whose marriages end typically face a dramatic economic downturn, which leads many women to poverty. In her ground-breaking work on American divorce, Weitzman (1985) found divorced women faced a 73% decline in their standard of living while their husband has a 42% rise (mostly because the woman usually gets care of the children). Another study found widowhood drops living standards by 18% and pushes 10% of women into poverty (Bound et al, 1991). Obviously other factors such as age, race and socioeconomic status play a role in determining poverty risk. These factors have been controlled for in the research, and yet, the marital status-poverty connection still persists (Dressel, 1988; Taeuber and Valdisera, 1986). As one woman aptly stated, "I'm one man away from poverty. If it wasn't for my husband I would be a bag lady" (Provincial Conference on Women and Aging, 1989).

The economic condition of older women, particularly widows, is closely tied to, even dependent upon, their husbands' financial status and/or longevity (Gee and Kimball, 1987). Underlying the domestic ideology, of course, is the economic ideology which reinforces women's economic dependence on men. The expectation that wives will be economically dependent in marriage is often played out in personal and family decisions that make it appear to be a self-fulfilling prophecy (Morgan, 1991). Wives' economic dependence increases as a consequence of incremental decisions not to seek further education, or to take part-time rather than full-time work [if they work at all] (Arendell, 1986). These findings are for middle-class women whose families could afford for her to leave the work-force. In many low-income families, the women may have worked outside the home continuously in low paying jobs.

"A vast majority of today's mature women conformed to the rules of the domestic ideology. Some remained at home and devoted their lives to the care of others, while some assumed a dual role of caregiver and employee. But regardless of the path they followed the rewards they receive in their later years are considerably less than those received by men" (Olson, 1990).

Lack of Education

A significant factor for the women over 65, in particular, is their low levels of education. 28% of the women aged 65–74, and 41% of the women over 75, had a grade eight education or less. When they were in their school years, education was not considered necessary since women were not expected to work outside the home. A common cliché of that era was that if a woman did go to university she was doing so to "get a man". The United Nations Educational, Scientific, and Cultural Organization (UNESCO) uses a benchmark of completion of grade nine to define functional illiteracy.

Without education women are forced to take low-paying jobs and these women may not have the knowledge needed in today's technological environment. If they must support themselves in the job market, they are at great disadvantage.

Impact of Caregiving

"The greatest barrier to economic equality for women is children" (Fuchs, 1989). This statement is true in that it is not the children themselves who create economic hardship for women, it is the societal structures for the care of children that are the problem. In one of the few longitudinal studies of older women, Moen (1985) found only 23% of the women studied had continuous full-time employment between 1972 and 1977. Most women had a combination of full and part-time work combined with periods out of the labour market. 30% of the women did not work at all during the period. Their workforce behavior was directly related to the needs of their children and aged parents. This discontinuous labour force pattern and uncounted and unpaid caregiving work has left older women with no or little pension income or retirement savings of their own (some women may have RRSPs in their name with money contributed by their husband). The pension system will be discussed in a later section.

"In my age, most women were single mothers, whether or not they had husbands."

Lauren

For those women who were in the labour force, their caretaking duties had definite economic costs. They were more likely to leave the labour force to care for their children, trade lower wages for the flexibility of part-time work, or have chosen jobs that offered flexible working conditions to accommodate their caregiving responsibilities (Kingson and O'Grady-LeShane, 1993; Stone et al, 1987). These effects further compounded the economic problems of the women who were single mothers, whether through widowhood, divorce or never being married.

Smith (1989) highlights the costs of motherhood in terms of fewer years of labour force participation and the reduction in wages associated with childrearing. An average woman who has two children is out of the labour force for an estimated 4.5 years and her lifetime earnings are substantially lower than those of women who do not have children (Smith, 1989; O'Rand and Landerman, 1984). This economic disadvantage is reflected in women's retirement income (Meyer, 1990). A U.S. study by Kingson and O'Grady (1993) found that each child raised was associated with a loss of $8 to $16 in a woman's monthly Social Security retirement benefit. These benefits have a similar structure to their Canadian counterparts; they are based on number of years in the labour force and income earned.

Women also care for their aging parents and for their aging spouses. Rimmer (1983) has characterized women's work as a caring cycle—women care for children, then care for parents or aged relatives, and then care for spouses. In a study of the work careers of retired women, Keating and Jeffrey (1983) found that 25% of married women had left the work force to care for a parent. Kingson and O'Grady-LeShane (1993) found that U.S. women who had left their last jobs to care for others (mostly parents) had monthly retirement benefits $127 less than women who had left the labour force voluntarily.

Gender Segregation of Occupations and Industries

The "domestic ideology" also defines women's relationship to the labour market: 1) women are secondary members of the labour market with marginal attachment, 2) women do not really have to work, but if they do, they work to earn "pin money" and 3) if women have to work, they work to supplement the family income (Olson, 1990). Although these are still heard today, for women over 55 the central message of their younger years was that their family role was most important and anything else was secondary.

These beliefs, backed by the corresponding economic theories, have led to gender segregation of the work force. Women have been, and are still, concentrated in five occupational groups—teaching, nursing or related health occupations, clerical, sales and service. Over half of women are concentrated in the low-paying clerical, sales (mostly retail) and service occupations (Statistics Canada, 1993). These figures would have been higher in the 1950 and 60's.

Women are also segregated by industry. Gee and Kimball (1987) apply the dual economy theory to women's segregated employment. There has been a transition in Western societies in the twentieth century from competitive capitalism—a system of many small and numerous firms, to one of monopoly capitalism—a system dominated by a fewer number of large corporations. This transition has not occurred equally in all industries. The *core sector* monopoly capitalism is more evident in the construction and extraction industries; and is less evident in the *peripheral sector* non-endurable manufacturing, agricultural, and retail trade industries. Industries in the core sector are large, unionized, and profitable and their workers make high salaries and have numerous benefits, such as private pension plans. Industries in the peripheral sector are smaller and non-unionized. Workers tend to make lower wages and do not have pension plans. Men are disproportionately found working in the core

"Before the seventies, nursing was not well paid. It was a struggle with four kids—I often had two night jobs so I could give my kids opportunities."

Lauren

"Women over 40 tend to be meek. We were raised that way—to never speak back to a man—'that's not polite.' Don't sit back and take what's handed to you—that's why we're here now."

Joan

sector while women are over-represented in the peripheral sector.

The Wage Gap

The segregation of women into low-paying industries and occupations results in a large wage gap between men and women, although it explains only part of the difference. Discrimination accounts for the rest. In 1991, women represented 20% of the workers in the 10 highest paid occupations. Men's overall average earnings were $79,463 while women's were $48,609. In the 10 lowest paid occupations, 72% of the workers were women. Men averaged $18,794, while women averaged $13,673. On average, Canadian women made 67.4% of men's full-time, full-year earnings in 1991, with Alberta women making 64.5% (Statistics Canada, 1993).

Education and marital status are the two most important factors in the wage gap. Single women with a university degree are approaching equality to men in pay and advancement prospects, but married women lag far behind. For example, single women with a university degree earn 92.8% of what men do, while their married counterparts earn only 68.7%. For women with high school graduation, single women earn 87.8% of what men do, while married women earn 63.4% (Crowley, 1993). This again shows the cost to women of the domestic ideology.

The majority of workers in low-paying occupations and industries are women. Most women employed in high-paying industries work in lower-paid occupations within those industries (i.e. clerical occupation in the oilpatch). Women who are in highly paid occupations are still paid significantly less than their male counterparts. Finally, women who are in traditionally highly paid occupations (such as manager) are increasingly employed in low-paying industries (service, retail).

Pension Plans—Not Designed for Women

"When I was married I didn't have to take the pension plan. Married women didn't have to contribute. When I had to, I spent the money on fixing the car or other things."

Lauren

All of the above factors are cumulative, they neatly build on one another, and their end result is low or no pension income for women. Canada has a three-tiered retirement income system which has institutionalized the domestic ideology. It was designed to provide a base-income support level (OAS and GIS) with the expectation that retirees will supplement this subsistence level with the Canada Pension Plan (the second tier) and investments, private pensions and savings (the third tier). The assumption underlying the system is that retirees are male who would hold full-time employment, live in stable nuclear families, would enjoy long marriages and a short retirement period with their dependent wives (Olson, 1990). Another assumption underlying the system is that women will be provided for by a man. How else would a housewife with thirty years of unpaid work get to the second or third tier?

The Canadian retirement income system discriminates against women in the following ways:

- because homemakers are not considered as workers they are not allowed to contribute to the Canada Pension Plan, and therefore are not entitled to receive retirement pensions. In 1990, only 62% of Canadian women were contributors to CPP (Statistics Canada, 1993).

- women are more likely to have to leave the labour force to care for children or aged parents. Their sporadic labour force participation results in lower CPP and private pension plan contributions, and therefore benefits. In fact, family responsibilities may cause women to miss out on the vesting privileges in private plans. In most private plans, the employer contributes a specified amount to the employee's plan. Vesting is when employer contributions are given to the employee when they leave the plan (usually when they quit). Each plan has rules to determine vesting privileges, they usually require the employee to be with the company at least five years.

- the Survivor's Pension under CPP is smaller than the benefits the widow's husband would have received had he lived.

- women are concentrated in occupations where there are few employer-sponsored pension plans. In 1990, 39% of all paid female workers were enrolled in employer-sponsored pension plans, up from 30.8% in 1980 (Statistics Canada, 1993). In addition, a woman's low wages result in inadequate benefits once she retires.

- women have consistently accounted for 70% of all part-time employment in Canada over the past 15 years (Statistics Canada, 1993). Most companies do not offer private pension plans to part-time workers (having to pay less benefits is a major reasons companies have increased their use of part-time workers).

Divorce also plays a role in the amounts of pension income women collect. The Canada Pension Plan does recognize that both spouses earn CPP credits equally during the time they live together, even if one of them was not in the paid labour force. This could result in a woman being eligible for certain CPP benefits she might not otherwise qualify for, or increase the amount of the benefit she receives. However, credit splitting is not automatic; it must be requested. Many women are not informed by their lawyers of this fact, nor are they informed that they may be entitled to part of their husband's private pension plan (Schmitz, 1991).

ALBERTA WOMEN AGED 35–55

The quotes in this section are from the women interviewed for this paper. Their profiles are at the back of the paper, pages 69–70.

This section will examine the current situation of Alberta women aged 35–55 (those who will become 55 in the next twenty years). Where relevant, the charts will include data from the women over the age of 55 to illustrate the changes that have taken place. The impact of the social changes of the last twenty years has been significant. These changes are, in some areas, dramatic.

DEMOGRAPHIC INFORMATION

Number of women and % of age group by age

Women are 49% of the population in the 35 to 55 age group.

Age	Number	% Women in Age Group
35 - 39	110,785	49
40 - 44	91,830	49
45 - 49	67,910	49
50 - 54	54,040	49

Source: Statistics Canada. Age, Sex and Marital Status. Ottawa: Supply and Services Canada, 1992. 1991 Census of Canada. Catalogue no. 93-310.

Location

The great majority of women in these age groups live in urban areas as well. More younger women live on rural farms as the chart shows and this peaks in the age 50–54 group.

Age Group	Urban Areas	Rural Farm	Rural non-farm
35-39	82%	6%	12%
40-44	80%	7%	13%
45-49	78%	9%	13%
50-54	78%	10%	13%

Source: Statistics Canada. Profile of urban and rural areas, Part A, Canada, Provinces and Territories. Ottawa: Industry, Science and Technology Canada, 1993. 1991 Census of Canada. Catalogue no. 93-339.

Ethnic Origin

The multi-cultural mix holds for the younger women.

Age Group	Canadian	British	French	European	Asian
25-44	4.49%	76.03%	12.85%	58.91%	7.62%
45-64	3.89%	63.31%	8.73%	52.43%	6.00%

Age Group	Arab	Latin, Central, South American	Caribbean	Inuit	Metis	North American Indian
25-44	0.64%	0.26%	0.19%	0.12%	2.00%	3.66%
45-64	0.35%	0.15%	0.19%	0.04%	1.17%	2.02%

Source: Statistics Canada. Ethnic Origin. Ottawa: Supply and Services Canada, 1992. 1991 Census of Canada. Catalogue no. 93-315.

> "You need to take these women who don't believe in themselves and nurture them so they feel they have something to offer. This takes time, money and energy."
>
> Paulette

Aboriginal women living in poverty face many barriers to employment—lack of education, lack of training and skills, early marriages and pregnancies, no previous work experiences, lack of coping skills, confidence and self-esteem (Native Employment Services, 1990).

Immigrant women are ghettoized in poorly paid labour market sectors, where they work as domestics, chambermaids, waitresses, sewing machine operators and building cleaners (Edmonton Immigrant Women, 1989). Many of these positions do not require the ability to speak English, which is a major factor preventing immigrant women from functioning fully in Canadian society.

Marital Status

Three-quarters of women in this age group are married. 10% of the women aged 35-39 are single (never married) which reflects the trend for women to marry later, or to opt for common-law partnerships.

Age Group	Single	Married	Separated	Widowed	Divorced
35-39	11%	73%	4%	1%	11%
40-44	7%	75%	4%	2%	12%
45-49	5%	75%	4%	3%	13%
50-54	4%	75%	3%	6%	12%

Source: Statistics Canada. Age, Sex and Marital Status. Ottawa: Supply and Services Canada, 1992. 1991 Census of Canada. Catalogue no. 93-310.

Common-law relationships are gaining in popularity. Between 1986 and 1991, there was a 50% increase in the number of Canadians living common-law. This increase is also reflected in the number of common-law families, which now account for 10% of all families in Canada. The majority (60%) of individuals in common-law relationships are under age 35. However, the rate of growth for living common-law for the over-35 age groups was higher than for the under-35 group. The following table shows the marital status of women living in common-law relationships.

Age Group	Single	Separated	Widowed	Divorced	Total
35-39	2%	1%	0%	3%	6%
40-44	1%	1%	0%	3%	5%
45-49	1%	0%	0%	3%	4%
50-54	0%	0%	1%	2%	3%

Source: Statistics Canada. Age, Sex and Marital Status. Ottawa: Supply and Services Canada, 1992. 1991 Census of Canada. Catalogue no. 93-310.

Number of Children

The fertility rate is dropping in Canada and in Alberta. This is shown clearly on the chart, where the majority of younger women have 2 or 3 children. Large families (with more than 5 children) now account for only 1% of Canadian families, while 40.7% of families have one child and another 40.3% have two children.

Age Group	None	1	2	3	4	5	6+
35-39	18%	14%	39%	20%	6%	2%	1%
40-44	14%	12%	41%	22%	8%	2%	2%
45-49	11%	11%	35%	26%	11%	4%	3%
50-54	10%	8%	26%	26%	16%	7%	6%

Source: Statistics Canada. Fertility. Ottawa: Supply and Services Canada, 1992. 1991 Census of Canada. Catalogue no. 93-321.

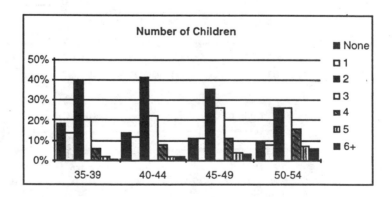

Living Arrangements—Private Households

The great majority of women live with their spouse, common-law partner or as a lone parent. There were 21,025 lone female parents in the 35–44 age group (10%) and 10,325 (9%) lone female parents in the 45–54 age group. This group is at a high risk for poverty as lone single parents have the lowest income of any family type. The incidence of low income for Alberta female lone parents was 48.4% in 1991, compared to 9.8% for husband-wife families.

Age Group	With Spouse, Common-law Partner or Lone parent	With Parent	With Related Family	With Non-related Family	With Relative	With Non Relative	Alone
35-44	90%	1%	1%	1%	1%	2%	6%
45-54	87%	1%	1%	0%	1%	2%	8%

Source: Statistics Canada. Families: Number, Type and Structure. Ottawa: Supply and Services Canada, 1992. 1991 Census of Canada. Catalogue No. 93-312.

Renting vs. Owning

Fewer women in these age groups are primary maintainers who own their own house. This may reflect the fact that more widows in the older age groups are primary maintainers. The low number of women who own their home may contribute to their poor financial situation in future.

Age Group	# of Female Primary Maintainers who Own	% of Women in Private Households who are Primary Maintainers
35-44	25,650	13%
45-54	18,205	15%

Source: Statistics Canada. Dwellings and Households. Ottawa: Supply and Services Canada, 1992. 1991 Census of Canada. Catalogue No. 93-311.

Collective Dwellings

A much smaller number of women in this age group are living in collective dwellings. The following table shows the distribution of women living in collective settings:

Age Group	Corrections Institution	Hospital	Special Care Homes	Other	Total
35-54	25	385	235	1,380	2,025

Note:
Hospital: more than a six-month stay in either general or psychiatric hospital
Special Care Home: includes nursing care homes, lodges, extended care centres
Other: includes religious orders, Hutterite colonies, rooming houses and hotels

Source: Statistics Canada. Dwellings and Households. Ottawa: Supply and Services Canada, 1992. 1991 Census of Canada. Catalogue No. 93-311.

Women with Disabilities

There is a significant percentage of younger women living in private households who have disabilities. Women with disabilities are a high risk group for financial difficulty, since they face additional barriers to education and employment. The older people get, the more disabilities they will develop, as is shown in the chart.

Age Group	With Disability	Total in Age Group	With Disability
35-44	16,305	202,615	8%
45-54	15,395	121,950	13%

Source: Statistics Canada. <u>Subprovincial Data for Alberta.</u> Ottawa: Supply and Services Canada, 1989. 1987 HALS Survey. Catalogue No. 82-611.

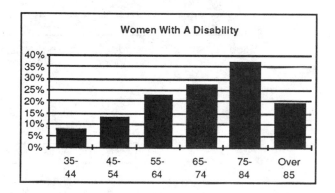

With respect to employment income, gender makes more difference than disability. The median employment income for Canadian females with a disability in 1985 was $8,360 compared to $19,250 for males with a disability. The corresponding median employment income for non-disabled females and males was $10,000 and $21,000 respectively (Harvey and Tepperman, 1990).

Education

The education levels for women have improved and are continuing to do so. Compared to their older counterparts, the women in the younger groups have more high school completions and more post-secondary education. This is a trend that is expected to continue. In 1991, 40% of Canadian women had some post-secondary education (up from 25% in 1981), with 10% having a university degree. Women presently make up the majority of undergraduate students in Canadian universities.

"When I went back to university full-time, my husband had his hours of work changed so he could be at home with the kids."

Paulette

Age	None	1-4 years	5-8 years	9-10 years	11-13 years	14-17 years	18 + years
35 - 44	0.25%	0.37%	3%	9%	49%	32%	7%
45 - 54	1%	1%	7%	17%	46%	24%	5%

Source: Statistics Canada. _Educational Attainment and School Attendance_. Ottawa: Supply and Services Canada, 1992. 1991 Census of Canada. Catalogue No. 93-328.

"My university degree made it easy to advance and I had lots of experience."

Lauren

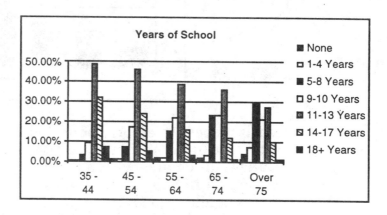

ECONOMIC INFORMATION

Total Income

About 45% of the women in both age groups are under the LICO for an urban area. 67% of women aged 35–44 earn less than $25,000, this rises slightly to 69% for the 45–54 age group. This again reflects their concentration in low-paying jobs or in part-time work (or both). In 1991, the average income for a female lone-parent family in Alberta was $25,407 in 1990 constant dollars, compared to $39,257 for male lone-parent families.

"You must have an arrangement with your husband where you have your own money. There must be some money you have complete control of."

Diana

Age Group	None	Under $9,999	$10,000-14,999	$15,000-24,999	$25,000-39,999	Over $40,000
35 - 44	9%	23%	13%	22%	21%	12%
45 - 54	9%	24%	13%	23%	19%	12%

Source: Statistics Canada. Selected Income Statistics. Ottawa: Supply and Services Canada, 1992. 1991 Census of Canada. Catalogue No. 93-331.

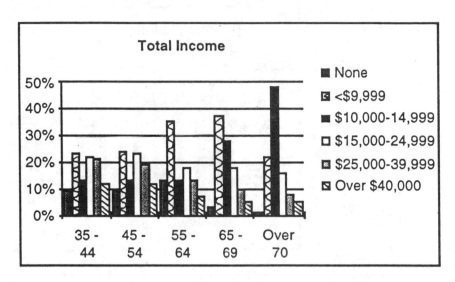

"I did hairdressing in my home, and sold cakes to get everyday money. My husband wouldn't give the kids (or me) an allowance."

Karen

Average and Median Incomes

The average incomes for these age groups are almost identical. While they are above the LICO for a woman with no children, they would place a woman in poverty status if she had to support children on these earnings.

	Average Incomes		Median Incomes	
Age	1985	1990	1985	1990
35 - 44	$20,612	$21,679	$17,842	$19,293
45 - 54	$19,914	$21,794	$16,559	$18,892

Source: Statistics Canada. Selected Income Statistics. Ottawa: Industry, Science and Technology Canada, 1993. 1991 Census of Canada. Catalogue # 93-331, 20% Sample Data.

Full-year, Full-time Employment Income and Marital Status

Average salaries in this category have increased for the younger women as shown on the chart. Single and divorced women make the highest income from full-year, full-time employment. The averages are much higher than those reflected in total income, since total income includes part-time work and income from government transfer payments.

Age Group	Single	Married	Separated	Widowed	Divorced	Average
35 - 44	$31,354	$26,949	$27,494	$27,214	$29,338	$27,638
45 - 54	$32,950	$25,729	$24,849	$25,649	$29,217	$26,473

Source: Statistics Canada. Selected Income Statistics. Ottawa: Supply and Services Canada, 1992. 1991 Census of Canada. Catalogue No. 93-331.

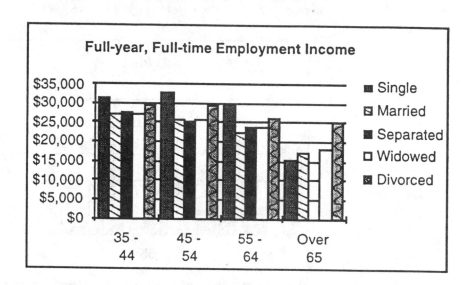

> "The push for women's equality is only part of the reason for the dramatic increase of women in the labour force. It's also a product of society's inexorable shift from a rural agrarian basis to one that's urban and industrial."
>
> Vanier Institute of the Family

Labour Force Participation Rates

Women's labour force participation rates have been increasing since 1971 in each age group, except the over 60. This is one of the most significant trends in Canada. Women made up 45% of the workforce in Canada in 1991, up from 36% in 1976. 53% of all women aged 15 and over were employed in 1991. Married women have accounted for almost all of the growth, with 56% of wives working. By 1990, dual-earner families made up 62% of all husband-wife families, up from 32% in 1967 and 55% in 1981. 63% of mothers with children less than age 16 were employed, with 57% of mothers with children under age 6 employed.

In Alberta, women age 25–44 had a labour force participation rate of 81% in 1991. The participation rate for women in this age group without children was 90%, while it was 74% for women with children.

Age Group	1971	1976	1981	1986	1991
35 - 44	49.6	59.0	68.1	76.6	82.5
45 - 54	51.6	56.6	61.9	70.2	78.6

Source: Statistics Canada. Labour Force Activity. Ottawa: Industry, Science and Technology Canada, 1993. 1991 Census of Canada. Catalogue # 93-324.

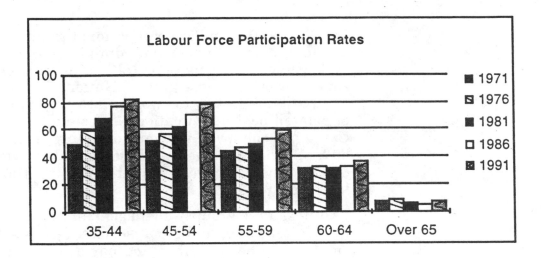

Occupation Groups

The following table shows the occupational groups, average incomes and the percentage of women in each group for Alberta women in 1991. The percentage of women employed in each group reflects the actual number of women working in that occupational group. The percentage of women in the occupational group reflects the proportion of women in each group.

Occupation Group	% of All Women Employed	Average Employment Income	% of Women in Group Employed Full-year, Full-time	Avg Employment Income for FT/FYR	% of Women in Occupation Group
Clerical	32%	$16,654	47%	$22,917	82%
Service	18%	9,799	30%	16,560	60%
Sales	10%	13,405	36%	22,189	47%
Management/ Administrative	9%	27,707	69%	31,732	36%
Medicine and Health	8%	24,222	43%	31,812	81%
Teaching	6%	24,676	46%	36,805	66%
Social Sciences	3%	21,401	46%	30,597	62%
Farming, horticultural	3%	9,606	49%	11,997	28%
Natural Sciences, Engineering and Mathematics	2%	28,818	62%	36,046	18%
Artistic/Recreational	1%	14,938	32%	24,401	47%
Processing	1%	14,349	41%	20,406	20%
Product Fabricating and Assembly	1%	13,861	46%	18,559	12%
Transportation	1%	15,673	37%	23,404	11%
Forestry	<1%	11,390	10%	22,241	11%
Mining	<1%	26,097	43%	41,024	3%
Construction	<1%	15,802	34%	24,905	3%

Source: Statistics Canada. Employment Income by Occupation. Ottawa: Industry, Science and Technology Canada, 1993. 1991 Census of Canada. Catalogue # 93-332.

In Alberta, the top five occupational groups are clerical, service, sales, management/administrative, and medical/health occupations. 77% of all employed women in Alberta work in these groups. Nationally, the top five occupational groups for women are teaching, clerical, nursing or related health occupations, sales and service. 71% of all Canadian employed women were represented in these groups. 60% of Alberta women work in clerical, service and sales occupations where average full-year, full-time salaries are less than $23,000.

The next four groups—management/administrative, medicine/health, teaching, and social services—account for 26% of all employed Alberta women and pay considerably more than the first three groups (all have average full-year, full-time salaries over $30,000). Women are the majority of the workers in the medicine/health (81%), teaching (66%) and social services (62%) occupational groups. As well, many women in management/ administrative jobs in Alberta work in these three occupational groups. This data is significant in light of current provincial government cutbacks in the areas of health, education and social services. Women are disproportionately affected by these cuts, and it is the well-paying jobs for women that are being lost.

In Canada, the percentage of women in non-traditional primary, manufacturing, construction, transportation, and materials handling jobs declined by 3% between 1981 and 1991. In 1991, 10% of employed women worked in these jobs, compared to 45% of employed men. In Alberta, less than 7% of women were employed in these jobs in 1991. Many provincial and federal government job creation programs centre on creating jobs in these areas. When governments speak of creating forestry, mining and construction jobs, they are speaking of creating jobs for men, not for women.

Less than half of women in most occupational groups worked full-year, full-time in 1991. Full-year, full-time employment is when a person works more than 30 hours each week for 49 to 52 weeks of the year. This can be accounted for by women's unemployment and mostly by part-time work. Part-time work was discussed previously, however it is important to note again the barriers facing women (especially those with children) from working and the resultant low earnings.

Women Farm Operators

In 1991, there were 745 Albertan women aged 35–55 who were sole farm operators, and 10,590 who were operators of farms with more than one operator. Women account for 29% of all farm operators aged 35–55 in Alberta. Women worked for pay off the farm an average of 178 days in 1991 (Statistics Canada, Agricultural Profile of Alberta, 1993).

WOMEN IN OTHER DEVELOPED COUNTRIES

The economic condition of women in other developed countries parallels that of women in Canada. Unless otherwise stated, all statistics here are from the United Nations (1991).

- Women are aging worldwide. In developed countries, more than half of women are over age 35, up from 32 years in 1972. In all developed countries, the proportion of women over the age of 60 is rising due to longer life expectancy and lower child-bearing rates. 24% of the female population in Germany is over 60, 19% in Japan, 22% in France, 26% in Sweden, 19% in the U.S., and 18% in Canada.

- Elderly women outnumber men everywhere. In Australia, New Zealand and Japan there are about 135 elderly women for every 100 elderly men. In Canada, there are 129 elderly women for every 100 elderly men.

- Changes affecting care for the elderly in all countries include longer life expectancy, increased divorce rates, and more women living alone. In Norway, one-third of women aged 67–74 had no one, either in the household or outside it, to ask for help.

- For women over age 60, more are widowed than married. In all developed countries the ratio of widows to widowers is about 4 to 1 and has remained stable over the last two decades. Overall, more than 50% of elderly women are not married.

- Woman-headed households tend to be poorer than those headed by men in all countries. Sweden has 27% of its households headed by women, France 22%, New Zealand 24%, the U.K. 25%, the U.S. 31%, and Canada 25%. Nearly half of the women heading households are elderly.

"Women make up half the world's population. They do two thirds of the world's work, they take home one-tenth of the world's pay, and they own one percent of the world's property."

United Nations

- Women's labour force participation rates rose in all countries between 1970 and 1990. The former U.S.S.R. had a rate of 60%, in Australia, Japan, and New Zealand 38% of the work force is women.

- Between 1970 and 1990, there was a large increase from 50 to 65% in the number of women aged 25–44 in the labour market in developed regions.

- Women fill well over half the clerical jobs everywhere. Within an occupational group, women are almost always in the less prestigious jobs. A study of 24 countries showed that many jobs such as typist, nurse and housekeeper were more than 90% female-occupied. A recent Swedish study found the same (Statistics Sweden, 1990).

- Women are paid less than men worldwide. Men are more likely to have regular full-time work and receive greater seniority and benefits. Women make 87% of what men do in Australia, 70% in the United Kingdom, 89% in France, 52% in Japan, 73% in Germany, and 67% in Canada.

- Very few women work in agriculture (5% or less) in many European countries. In the U.S., this number is declining.

- Services employ 80% or more of women in Norway, the Netherlands, Sweden and the U.S.

- On average about 13% of women are self-employed in the developed countries.

PROGRAMS

Programs that have been successful and that could be adapted to Alberta will be reviewed here. Some of the most innovative programs originated in the Third World. Many women in North America are similar to their Third World counterparts—low on capital, low on technology and labour-intensive.

Granny Flats

These are self-contained, pre-fabricated units which can sit independently or be attached to a house. They can be moved from one site to another which greatly saves on building costs. They allow families to provide accommodation to their elder members while maintaining the privacy and lifestyle of each party. Granny flats are widely in use in Australia and New Zealand. Rents are usually not more than 20% of a person's income; government subsidies pay the remaining costs. The units are the size of a two-car garage and are self-contained with a living room, bedroom, kitchen and bathroom (Lazarowich, 1990).

Gifted Housing

In the United Kingdom, an organization has developed a program called Gifted Housing to deal with large under-inhabited houses and the need for additional housing for the elderly. People owning larger homes donate them to the non-profit organization, which then converts them into rental apartments for other elderly people. In exchange, the donor lives rent-free in one of the units for the rest of their lives. It frees them from property taxes and maintenance costs while providing them with companionship and emergency assistance.

Small Group Housing

A small number of unrelated older adults share an ordinary residential setting in this type of program. The type of support in each home varies, from staff providing meals and household maintenance, to where the tenants do most of this work. These homes are popular in the U.K. and parts of the U.S. The "fit" of the people in the house is crucial if it is to succeed.

Co-housing

Co-housing projects are where the expenses of building and maintaining a house are shared among a group of people. It makes it possible for lower-income people to afford to buy a single-family dwelling. Homeowners buy land, choose the architect, and plan the building of homes and community centres on a consensus basis. Each family agrees to split the cost of land, roads, septic systems, and the water supply and for architectural, survey and engineering fees. People share laundry facilities, lawn mowers, snow blowers, etc. which reduces the money each household must spend. Co-housing projects are limited equity cooperatives; each family pays a mortgage and taxes to the cooperative which then pays the bills. Co-housing combines the financial and social advantages of cooperative housing while allowing members to own their home and build equity, which is especially important for women. Co-housing is common in Denmark and over 100 projects are underway in the U.S.

Rural Women's Programs

In Australia, there are programs in place to overcome the disadvantages attached to various kinds of isolation by improving information, education and employment opportunities. The Rural Women's Access Grants Program provides grants to community groups to implement employment services, education and training projects. Another program provides hostel accommodation to enable students from remote locations to continue their education.

High-school Apprenticeship Programs

These programs allow students to learn a trade such as carpentry or machinist while continuing to earn high school credits. They are modelled after the European apprenticeship system where people begin apprenticing at much younger ages than Canadians. These programs, such as Ontario's School Workplace Apprenticeship Program (SWAP), enable young adults to combine their educations. Students graduate with a trade and a diploma. These programs could be a good way to encourage young women to enter non-traditional (for women) trades.

Policies to Increase Wages

These policies include minimum wage legislation, pay equity, and fair wages in government contracts. There is great controversy over whether these programs help or hurt the working poor. They are more likely to hurt the working poor when:

- there are other good substitutes for higher-priced labour (i.e. there are many unemployed people who will work for low wages)
- employers cannot pass along the increased costs to consumers without having their sales decline
- labour costs are a substantial portion of total costs (Gunderson et al, 1990).

It has been argued that adverse employment effects may not occur due to the following:

- labour markets may not behave in the competitive fashion suggested by the economics textbooks, given the other non-competitive factors such as monopoly, unionization and administered pricing
- wage increases may shock management into more efficient practices and cost savings elsewhere
- wage increases may increase productivity and reduce absenteeism
- it may be socially desirable to not support the low-wage industries where jobs are likely to be lost (Gunderson et al, 1990).

Pay equity has been ineffective for women since they are segregated in low-paying jobs. Equal pay for work of equal value is designed to compare dissimilar occupations as long as they are of comparable value. It has the potential to correct the pay inequity created by the fact that female jobs are often undervalued.

These practices are institutionalized in the European Community and in the Federal government here. These measures directly challenge the economic structures and therefore generate tremendous resistance. The fact that they have had a small impact so far is due to the type of legislation and the resistance to implementing them, and does not mean they will not improve women's economic situation over time.

Cooperative Childcare Programs

An example of this program is the Joyland Child Development Centre in Auburn, Alabama. It is a non-profit, grassroots program that provides not only childcare but trains and hires the mothers as childcare workers, encourages them to continue their education, and counsels them on job-hunting and solving financial problems. Most of the mothers work during the day at fast-food or clerical jobs and go to school at night. They are subsidized by the state and the mothers pay fees for childcare.

Savings Clubs

Women in the Third World have long had savings clubs where they pool their weekly savings and make loans to each other. Savings clubs in Sri Lanka, India, and Bangladesh have remarkable track records for helping members meet emergencies, start small businesses and reach out to empower other women. Several programs have started in the U.S. Basic requirements are that the women be from the same socioeconomic class, they hold their money in a common fund, have provisions to advance loans, have income-generating activities, engage in some form of community action, develop their own rules, and share leadership. It is obvious they are gaining much more than financial expertise. Some clubs focus only on financing women's business start-up costs.

Microenterprise Development

Another Third World export, known as microenterprise development and microcredit lending, uses funds from socially conscious investors to make loans to enable the poor to become self-employed and self-sufficient. The most famous program is the Grameen Bank in Bangladesh, which employs 12,000 people, serves almost a million borrowers and has lent more than $300 million. The close collaborative relationship the bank has established with its loan recipients has resulted in repayment rates between 98 and 99%. The concept of peer-group lending, which makes borrowers accountable to one another as well as to the bank for loan repayments, is what is responsible for much of its success. There are many micro-lending programs in the U.S. including the Lakota Fund, which has funded native women in taking over the "middleman" distribution of their crafts and the Good Faith Fund in Arkansas, which gives entrepreneurial training and support to women launching their own businesses.

Education Groups

After the Nairobi conference for International Year of the Woman, women in the developed countries in particular realized how they must become informed about economic theory and practice. There have been several groups set up where women can network and articulate their economic concerns in both academic and popular language. DAWN (Development Alternatives for Women for a New Era), a group of women from Southern countries, is working to formulate an economic model as if women matter. The Women's Alternative Economic Network (WAEN) in the U.S. brings popular educators, grass-roots organizers, labour activists and church women together to learn and share techniques for teaching "economic literacy."

PROJECTIONS

In this section the major trends which will affect women over the next twenty years will be examined. The most significant trend is the shift to the knowledge or information economy—this underlies most of the changes we are witnessing today. Another major trend, independent of the former, is the aging of the population in Canada and in the Western world. In any time of great change there are both devastating consequences and exciting opportunities. The threats and opportunities for women will be highlighted for each trend.

The "Graying" of Society

The proportion of the population which is elderly (those over age 65) is expected to increase dramatically as the baby boom begins to reach old age around 2010. Most of the women now aged 35–55 will become 65 before this increase. An aging society has implications for the costs associated with social programs and for the ability of the working population to finance social expenditure (Burke, 1991). Social spending can be expected to increase because of higher pension and health care costs. According to the Organization for Economic Development (OECD), within the next fifty years half of all Canada's social spending will be on the elderly. There is much disagreement over whether these costs can be borne without higher taxes or reduced social programs. Future capacity to finance these expenses will be affected by the rate of real growth in the economy, the number of employed people and their real earnings, and the real rate of increase in benefits. Ivan Fellegi, Chief Statistician for Statistics Canada, predicts that should Canada maintain economic growth at the rate experienced over the last 50 years "we should be able to support the cost of an aging society."

Opportunities

- the increasing numbers of older persons will create new markets for products designed for their needs—new industries will appear and services and products will improve.
- women are the majority of service providers to the elderly, both formally and informally—there will be increased demand for these services.

Threats

- there is worry (and much disagreement) over whether there will be enough money in the OAS and CPP funds to pay people when they reach old age.
- this trend has been used by some economists and governments as a reason to reduce or cut social programs, this disproportionately affects women.
- with the above, there have been attempts to create conflict between the generations by saying the elderly are taking away scarce resources from the young—this could further ageist stereotypes and increase abuse of the elderly. Since the majority of elderly are women and the majority of abuse victims are women, elderly women have an increased risk for abuse.

Continuing Increase of Women in the Workforce

The presence of women working in the workforce is anticipated to increase to where the levels of men and women are equal. There are many implications of this major change in the country's social fabric.

Opportunities

- as women achieve higher education levels and move into male-dominated occupations their earnings will increase.
- increased participation in the workforce means more women will be contributing to private pension plans. Women are also saving more money in their own RRSPs. This will increase their chances of having adequate income in retirement.
- the trend in part-time work and contracting out may result in part-time workers demanding, and governments passing, legislation for adequate benefits and pension plans.

Threats

- society's structures have not kept up with the changes in society. This is evident in the lack of adequate childcare and the dual work demands placed on women. Childcare is one of the most significant barriers keeping women from attaining education and well-paying employment. Women's workforce participation is still being trivialized by the claim that more women are working because the family needs the money—an extension of the "pin-money" myth. While this may be true for many women, the fact remains that they have few choices in being able to have paid work and raise children (since unpaid childcare is not "work").

- the opportunities created by increased participation do not apply equally to all women. Elderly, lesbian, disabled, aboriginal and other visible minority women face continuing discrimination, and lone mothers continue to be mostly poor.

- there is an increasing polarity between rich and poor women which could create difficulties in having a unified women's movement.

THE SHIFT TO THE KNOWLEDGE ECONOMY

Whether they call it the knowledge society, the information age or post-capitalist society, the experts and non-experts alike agree something is radically changing our world. That "something" is technology. It is not approaching in the future, it has been here for the last ten years (at least). Its effects are wide-ranging: radical changes in management methods, the rise in micro businesses, the shift in hours of work, governments caught with large debt loads, and shortages in skilled knowledge workers.

"You're definitely in the Death Valley of the job market when at least three-quarters of the workers are men (old economy industries tend to be male-dominated). That may sound like an odd indicator, but the simple fact is that in the new economy—the one with all the growth prospects, the big salaries and the security—women account for 48.4% of the knowledge intensive jobs.'

Nuala Beck

These trends are structural changes in society and the economy. The major threat to women, and to society in general, is scarcity thinking. The focus of scarcity thinking is that there is not enough and on what is wrong, instead of what is working and how much there is. There are more opportunities for women now than there may have ever been in history. Women must find them. The key to success in this new economy is not only having knowledge or information, but lies in being able to put that knowledge into practice.

The largest threat to society is the lack of knowledge about the knowledge economy. Economic theory as we know it is obsolete—it cannot count the new economic growth (women know that counting has never been a strong point of economics). Governments and business continue to make decisions based on outdated economics, causing many of the problems we now have. The greatest opportunities will come to those who quickly learn the rules of the new game.

Changes in Management Practices

There has been a major shift in business away from rigid, hierarchical structures to networked structures. Empowerment is the new management buzz-word (feminists have been talking about empowerment for years—these women are well prepared for the new management!). **The emphasis in the new structures is on sharing information, not hoarding it—teams, cooperation, creativity and initiative are the values.** Reengineering (re-designing work to use technology efficiently and to gain stated results) is reshaping the workplace. Technology is allowing more flexibility in work schedules, people can work from anywhere (including home) and stay connected with the office by modem and portable computer.

Opportunities

- workplaces are finally beginning to realize that it is their *structure* that makes it seem as if women are less committed to work because of their family responsibilities. Flex-time, shorter work-weeks and in-house day care are being implemented. These changes are "humanizing" the workplace and will help women remain in the labour force while raising children.
- women as a group are already familiar with the new structures and can adapt quickly to them—this may give them an advantage over men in the work place.

Threats

- reengineering has the potential to decimate clerical jobs— in some new structures there are no clerical jobs since everyone does their own copying and word processing. This could be disastrous for the bulk of women trained as clerical workers if they do not receive retraining.
- working from home will continue to burden women with dual work responsibilities and may give governments an excuse to not implement childcare programs.
- working from home can increase women's isolation (a risk factor for wife abuse) and enable employers to lower pay and benefits, as is currently being done in the textile industry where piece work done at home is paid at subsistence levels.

The Rise of The Woman Business Owner

The key word for business structure in the knowledge economy is micro. Smaller businesses that are flexible and adaptable will become the norm. Women own and operate nearly one third of all small businesses in Canada. The number of self-employed women increased by 265% over the last two decades (compared to 74% for men). Faith Popcorn, a trend forecaster sees a trend she calls "female-think" and she expects that in ten years women will run more companies than are in the Fortune 500 now. She finds that the computer is giving women greater opportunity to quit office jobs and start their own businesses (Canadian Press, 1994).

Another trend is identified by Drucker (1993) in his book Post-Capitalist Society. "Outsourcing" is contracting out all the activities that take away from an organization's main work. For example, a hospital contracting out janitorial activities or a law firm hiring someone else to maintain their library. These activities tend to have poor productivity since management has no interest or expertise in them. Drucker argues that workers who do not perform the main work of an organization are not valued and will never be promoted. This is certainly the case for most clerical workers. However, if a clerical worker was employed by a company that specialized in clerical work, she would be a valued employee and would have opportunities for advancement. Outsourcing, or contracting out, will occur in many activities where women are the majority of workers.

Opportunities
- outsourcing can give more women opportunities to start their own businesses where their work is valued (valued work is well paid work) and there is room for advancement.
- 48% of home-based businesses are located outside cities— rural women can now access the entire world market through computer. This can create many opportunities for rural women.
- self-employment can allow many women to integrate childcare with their work on their own terms.

Threats
- more jobs may be lost from outsourcing than are replaced, due to increased productivity. Companies that are managed and staffed by people knowledgeable in their line of work know how to get that work done as efficiently as

possible. This may result in fewer workers needed to accomplish the same amount of work.

Is this Part-time Work—or is it the New Full-time Work?

Full-time work has traditionally been viewed as 40 hours per week. The trend towards part-time work is global; among developed countries one in seven workers holds a part-time job. There has been much interest in Canada and Europe in a shortened work week in response to massive job lay-offs. Bell Canada in Quebec just completed a deal with their employees to shorten work hours so no one will be laid off. Germany is seriously considering moving to a four day work-week.

Opportunities
- no one has been able to come up with a way to pay women who work full-time in the home. As has been shown throughout this paper, women who do not have their own adequate income run the risk of poverty their entire lives. Women who work outside the home are often exhausted from doing two jobs (women still do most housework). Women who want to work outside the home and spend time with their children currently have few choices. O'Hara (1993), outlines the benefits of working fewer hours to individuals, society and the environment in his book Working Harder Isn't Working. O'Hara recommends starting with a four day work-week and moving gradually to a twenty hour work-week, without much loss in standard of living. This is revolutionary thinking—and may hold a key to many of the economic problems women face. This would allow both spouses to be financially independent and to spend more time with their families. This concept needs to be seriously studied by women.

Threats
- many companies have created part-time work to lower wages and to get around paying benefits—women are 70% of part-time workers and many of them cannot afford to be.
- changing the work-week norm would require government support and legislation, always a slow process—in the mean time women are without good pay and benefits.

Continued Decrease of Government Spending and Deficit Reduction

As both federal and provincial governments tackle their deficits, social programs will continue to be cut. This hits women hard as they are the main recipients of social benefits.

Opportunities
- women have been well-mannered and quiet about their poverty—if pushed far enough it may push them to organize and develop a politically strong voice—their numbers will make them a voting force.
- the lack of government funding may force women's organizations to develop new ways of financing themselves—this would give them the freedom to express themselves without fear of losing their government funding.

Threats
- cuts to, or elimination of, education finance programs (student loans and grants) and programs for training women will make it more difficult for "non-rich" women to attain the skills needed for well-paying employment.
- more women and children will not have their basic needs met and will be living in severe poverty. The severity of their poverty defines their ability to escape from their poverty.
- more women will be forced to turn to illegal means (such as prostitution) to meet basic survival needs.

Shortage of Skilled Labour

The labour force has absorbed most of the baby boom generation and there will be fewer young people entering the labour force. Canada wide labour shortages are predicted by the mid to late 1990's in some areas. The shortage of qualified labour could be the largest impediment to economic growth. Employers are seeking "knowledge workers" who offer computing and technological skills and experience and trades workers, both of whom are currently in shortage (Stoffman, 1993).

Opportunities
- the demand for labour may create opportunities for women and immigrants as these are the two main sources of new labour in Canada.

Threats
- jobs will increasingly be split into high-skilled, well-paying and low-paying, unskilled "McJobs"(O'Hara, 1993)—many women do not have the education and skills which will be in demand.
- training programs are not training women in jobs with a well-paid future and existing government training programs have been found to be mostly ineffective (CBC, 1994).

THE FUTURE...

In her book Shifting Gears, Nuala Beck (1993) is already predicting the next economic movement—the E circle. E is for engineering and the main engines of growth will be genetic engineering and biotechnology, artificial intelligence, space and new materials development. The only constant left in the economy is constant change. The opportunities are more than abundant for those who have vision and can plan for the future now. Women have the skills and the knowledge to lead the way.

RESEARCHER'S RECOMMENDATIONS

In addition to the Council;'s recommendations, the researcher recommends the following:

1. That a series of province-wide meetings be held for women to meet each other and brainstorm solutions to their economic situations and where information on innovative programs could be provided. This could be the seed for forming savings clubs, microenterprise developments, childcare pooling and political advocacy in women's communities. That recommendations coming out of these meetings be distributed throughout the province and follow-up work be done to assist in planning future action.

2. That a national conference on Economics and Women be sponsored by an agency(s) in Alberta. This would draw national media attention and generate knowledge and recommendations to take back to communities.

3. That "granny flat" and shared housing be considered by agencies dealing with low income women to provide housing and support.

4. That regional meetings be held among agencies serving women to discuss economics and brainstorm solutions. The goal would be to co-ordinate some of the recommendations in this report.

PROFILES OF THE WOMEN INTERVIEWED

Five women were interviewed for this paper, they were selected to present as diverse a group as possible. To protect their identities, their names, and certain details of their situations, have been changed. These brief biographies do not in any way capture the richness of these women's stories. Their words, in the quotes throughout this paper, do reveal their strength in coping with difficult situations, their humour, and their wisdom.

Lauren

"Having a sense of humour has gotten me through. Also having a wide circle of friends and interests outside of work."

58 years old. Ukrainian in background, Lauren did not speak English until age 5. She completed her nursing degree after high school and worked throughout Alberta. Lauren has worked continuously, both part-time and full-time, depending on her family commitments. After her divorce, she was sole supporter of her four children. Lauren held nursing management jobs, mostly on the night shift as it paid better and allowed her to be at home with her children during the day. Lauren is currently a manager.

Karen

"I always said when I was a child 'When I get grown up, I'm going to England.' And I did when I was eighteen."

58 years old. Currently living in a small, southern town. Raised on a rural farm, Karen was one of thirteen children. Their father died when she was young, as a result the family was very poor. Because of their poverty, Karen went to work at an early age and did not complete high school. She eventually got her hairdresser's certificate. Karen ran several small businesses before her marriage, but afterwards her husband did not want her to have her own business. She has three children. Karen is currently experiencing much difficulty with legal proceedings of her divorce. This process has been emotionally difficult and financially draining. Her husband is unwilling to settle their joint finances. Karen is working part-time in a service job.

Joan

"After all the years of working and raising the children, now I can't sit still. It drives everyone nuts!"

58 years old. Currently living in St. Albert. Joan was raised on a farm in rural Saskatchewan. She was married after becoming pregnant in high school. She and her husband moved to B.C. and then to Alberta. They had two more children before Joan divorced her husband. Because she could not afford a lawyer, Joan received no support from her husband. She moved to Edmonton with her children and worked as a cook. She then went back to school for her high school and business diploma through a Manpower program. She has worked in clerical jobs since, and is currently employed as a client aide.

Diana

"I never fit into that mold. I hated cooking and baking. I was a poor housewife, I had to get out of the house."

65 years old, currently living in Edmonton. Diana and her family immigrated to Canada when she was fifty. Before immigrating, she ran her own business for 15 years. In Canada, she began with clerical jobs while she learned the culture, and eventually moved into management positions. Diana is currently working in a social service agency and wants to continue working or volunteering.

Paulette

"You need money to survive, but you have to like what you're doing and be okay with yourself and who you are. For women it can be hard to know who you are, apart from work, your partner and your kids."

35 years old, currently living in St. Albert. Of Native descent, Paulette was raised in urban Alberta. She finished high school and volunteered in working with children, which led to a full-time job. She then went back to college for her social work diploma. She married and worked part-time while pregnant with her first child. After the birth of her second child, she began home study through Athabasca University for her social work degree. She then went full-time to University to complete her degree. Paulette and her husband co-own a business which allows them to share childcare duties.

REFERENCES

Aburdene, Patricia and Naisbitt, John. 1992. *Megatrends for Women*. New York: Random House.

Alberta Community Development. 1994. *News Release*. Edmonton: Government of Alberta.

Alberta Status of Women Action Committee. 1991. *Women Against Poverty*. Edmonton.

Arendell, Terry. 1987. Women and the economics of diversity in the contemporary United States. *Signs*. 13:121-35.

Badgett, M.V. and Williams, Rhonda. 1992. The economics of sexual orientation: Establishing a research agenda. *Feminist Studies*. 18:649-657.

Baumol, William; Blinder, Alan; and Scarth, William. 1988. *Economics Principles and Policy*. Toronto: Harcourt Brace Jovanich.

Beck, Nuala. 1992. *Shifting Gears: Thriving in the New Economy*. Toronto: HarperCollins.

Blakely, Mary Kay. 1992. Quilting new networks. *Ms*. March/April:19-23.

Bound, John; Duncan, Greg; Laren, Deborah; and Oleinick, Lewis. 1991. Poverty dynamics in widowhood. *Journal of Gerontology*. 46:S115-124.

Burke, Mary Anne and Spector, Aron. 1991. Falling through the cracks:Women aged 55-64 living on their own. *Perspectives on Labour and Income*. Winter:14-17.

Burke, Mary Anne. 1991. Implications of an aging society. *Canadian Social Trends*. Spring:6-8.

Canadian Press. 1994. Women top entrepreuners, trend seer Faith Popcorn says. *Edmonton Journal*. February 5:C2.

CBC. 1994. *Venture*. Jan. 30.

Chawla, Raj. 1991. Dependency ratios. *Canadian Social Trends*. Spring:3-5.

Choi, Namkee. 1992. Correlates of the economic status of widowed and divorced elderly women. *Journal of Family Issues*. 13:38-54.

CLMPC Task Forces on the Labour Force Development Strategy. 1990. *A Survey of Policies and Programs for Older Workers in Other Industrialized Nations*. Ottawa: CLMPC.

Coen, Diane and Stanley, Guy. 1993. *Class Action: Making the Future Work-Now!* Montreal: Davies.

Cote, Michel. 1991. Visible minorities in the Canadian labour force. *Perspectives on Labour and Income.* Summer:17-25.

Crompton, Susan. 1993. Facing retirement. *Perspectives on Labour and Income.* Spring:31-38.

Crowley, Brian Lee. 1993. Does counting bodies add up to fairness? *Canadian Business.* November:71-78.

Dressel, Paula. 1988. Gender, race, and class: beyond the feminization of poverty in later life. *Gerontologist.* 28:177-80.

Drucker, Peter. 1993. *Post-Capitalist Society.* New York: HarperBusiness.

Easterlin, R.; MacDonald, C.; and Macunovich, D. 1990. Retirement prospects of the baby boom generation: A different perspective. *The Gerontologist.* 30:776-783.

England, Paula. 1993. The separative self: androcentric bias in neoclassical assumptions. In *Beyond Economic Man*, ed. Marianne A. Ferber and Julie A. Nelson, 37-53. Chicago: University of Chicago Press.

Even, W. and NacPherson, D. 1990. The gender gap in pensions and wages. *Review of Economics and Statistics.* 71:259-265.

Ferber, Marianne and Nelson, Julie. 1993. Introduction: the social construction of economics and the social construction of gender. In *Beyond Economic Man*, ed. Marianne A. Ferber and Julie A. Nelson, 1-22. Chicago: University of Chicago Press.

Frank, Robert. 1988. *Passions Within Reason: The Strategic Role of the Emotions.* New York: W.W. Norton.

Frenken, Hubert. 1991. Women and RRSPs. *Perspectives on Labour and Income.* Winter:8-13.

Frenken, Hubert and Maser, Karen. 1992. Employer-sponsored pension plans - who is covered? *Perspectives on Labour and Income.* Winter:27-33.

Fuchs, V.R. 1989. Women's quest for economic equality. *Journal of Economic Perspectives on Labour and Income.* 3:25-41.

Galarneau, Diane. 1991. Women approaching retirement. *Perspectives on Labour and Income.* Autumn:28-39.

Ghalam, Nancy Zukewich. 1993. *Women In the Workplace*. Ottawa: Statistics Canada, Ministry of Industry, Science and Technology.

Goldenburg, Susan. 1991. *Global Pursuit: Canadian Business Strategies for Winning in the Borderless World*. Whitby: McGraw-Hill Ryerson.

Goldscheider, Frances. 1990. The aging of the gender revolution. *Research on Aging*. 12:531-545.

Gunderson, Morley; Muszynski, Leon; and Keck, Jennifer. 1990. *Women and Labour Market Poverty*. Ottawa: Canadian Council on the Status of Women.

Hardy, Melissa and Hazelrigg, Lawrence. 1993. The gender of poverty in an aging population. *Research on Aging*. 15:243-278.

Harvey, Edward and Tepperman, Lorne. 1990. *Selected Socio-economic Consequences of Disability for Women in Canada*. Special Topic Series from The Health and Activity Limitation Survey. Ottawa: Industry, Science and Technology. Statistics Canada Catalogue # 82-615, Vol. 2.

Hatch, Laurie. 1990. Effects of work and family on women's later-life resources. *Research on Aging*. 12:311-338.

Keating, N. and Jeffrey, B. 1983. Work careers of ever married and never married retired women. *Social Security Bulletin*. 43:416-421.

Kerstetter, Steve. 1991. Pensions. In *Aging into the 21st Century*, ed. Christine Blais, 331-336. North York: Captus University Publications.

Killean, Elmer. 1986. *Equality in the Economy: A Synthesis of the Proceedings of a Workshop*. Montreal: Institute for Research on Public Policy.

Kingson, Eric and O'Grady-LeShane, Regina. 1993. The effects of caregiving on women's social security benefits. *The Gerontologist*. 33, 2:230-239.

Lazarowich, Micheal. A review of the Victoria, Australia granny flat program. *The Gerontologist*. 30:171-177.

Lipsey, Richard; Purvis, Douglas; and Steiner, Peter. 1991. *Economics*. New York: Harpercollins.

Maki, Dennis and Ng, Ignace. 1990. Effects of trade unions on the earnings differential between males and females: Canadian evidence. *Canadian Journal of Economics*. 23:305-311.

Marshall, Katherine. 1994. Balancing work and family responsibilities. *Perspectives on Labour and Income on Labour and Income.* Spring:26-30.

McGee, Ellen and Kimball, Meredith. 1987. *Women and Aging.* Toronto: Butterworths.

McLaughlin, Diane and Jensen, Leif. 1993. Poverty among older Americans: The plight of nonmetropolitan elders. *Journal of Gerontology.* 48:S44-54.

Meyer, M.H. 1990. Family status and poverty among older women: The gendered distribution of retirement income in the United States. *Social Problems.* 37:551-563.

Minkler, Meredith. 1989. Gold in gray:reflections on business' discovery of the elderly market. *The Gerontologist.* 29:17-23.

Moen, Phyllis. 1985. Unemployment, public policy, and families: forecasts for the 80's. *Journal of Marriage and the Family.* 45:751-60.

Morgan, Leslie. 1991. *After Marriage Ends: Economic Consequences for Mid-life Women.* Newbury Park: Sage.

Mori, Monica and McNern, Janet. 1991. *Women and Aging: An Annotated Bibliography.* Vancouver: Simon Fraser University Gerontology Research Centre.

National Action Committee on the Status of Women. 1992. *Review of the Situation of Women in Canada 1992.* Ottawa.

Ng, Edward. 1992. Children and elderly people: Sharing public income and resources. *Canadian Social Trends.* Summer:12-15.

Nusberg, Charlotte; Gibson, Mary Jo; and Peace, Sheila. 1984. *Innovative Aging Programs Abroad: Implications for the U.S.* Westport: Greenwood Press.

O'Bryant, Shirley and Morgan, Leslie. 1989. Financial experience and well-being among mature widowed women. *The Gerontologist.* 29:245-251.

O'Hara, Bruce, 1993. *Working Harder Isn't Working.* Vancouver: North Star Books.

O'Rand, A. and Landerman, R. 1984. Women's and men's retirement income: Early family role effects. *Research on Aging.* 6:25-44.

Olson, Paulette. 1990. Mature women and the rewards of domestic ideology. *Journal of Economic Issues.* 24:633-643.

Ontario Advisory Council on Women's Issues. 1991. *Raising the Issues: A Discussion Paper on Aging Women in Ontario.* Toronto.

Pesando, J.; Gunderson, M.; and McLaren, J. 1991. Pension benefits and male-female wage differentials. *Canadian Journal of Economics.* 24:536-550.

Pillanger, Jane. 1992. *Women's Pay and Employment in the European Community.* London: MacMillan.

Provincial Conference on Aging. 1989. *Report on Women: Midlife and Beyond: Provincial Conference on Aging, Oct. 18-19, 1989.* Winnipeg: Manitoba Council on Aging; Manitoba Women's Directorate.

Rimmer, L. 1983. The economics of work and caring. In *A Labour of Love: Women, Work and Caring*, ed. J. Finch and D. Grove, 131-147. London: Routledge and Kegan Paul.

Rix, Sara. 1990. Who pays for what? Ensuring financial security in retirement. In *Pre-retirement Planning for Women: Program Design and Research*, ed. Christopher Hayes and Jane Deren, 5-26. New York: Springer.

Rose, Kalima. 1992. *Where Women are Leaders: The SEWA Movement in India.* London: Zed Books.

Schmitz, C. 1991. Ex-wives lose millions by failing to claim split of ex-husband's Canada Pension Plan credits. *The lawyers weekly*. Vol. 10, No. 44:1,14.

Semler, Ricardo. 1993. Worker's paradise? *The Globe and Mail Report on Business.* December:38-48.

Seniors Advisory Council for Alberta. 1992. *Older Albertans.* Edmonton:Seniors Advisory Council of Alberta.

Shao, Maria. 1994. Thinking on her feet: Out of rape and recovery, comes shoe company with a conscience. *Edmonton Journal.* February 22:C1.

Siroonian, James. 1993. Investment income of Canadians. *Perspectives on Labour and Income.* Summer:53-59.

Smith, J.P. 1989. Women, mothers and work. In *Women's Life Cycle and Economic Insecurity*, ed. M. Ozawa, 42-70. New York: Praeger.

Smith, Joan. 1987. Comparable worth, gender and human capital theory. In *Ingredients for Women's Employment Policy*, ed. Christine Bose and Glenna Spitze, 233-239. Albany: State University of New York Press.

Sparr, Pamela. 1992. How we got into this mess and ways to get out. *Ms*. March/April:29-36.

Spector, Aron. 1992. Measuring Low Incomes in Canada. *Canadian Social Trends*. Summer:8-10.

Statistics Canada. 1993. *Agricutural Profile Of Alberta - Part 2*. Ottawa: Ministry of Industry, Science and Technology. 1991 Census of Canada. Catalogue No. 95-383.

Statistics Canada. 1993. *The Daily: The Violence Against Women Survey*. Ottawa: Ministry of Industry, Science and Technology.

Stoffman, Daniel. 1993. Working class heroes. *The Globe and Mail Report on Business*. December:51-62.

Strassmann, Diana. 1993. Not a free market: the rhetoric of disciplinary authority in economics. In *Beyond Economic Man*, ed. Marianne A. Ferber and Julie A. Nelson, 54-68. Chicago: University of Chicago Press.

Taeuber, Cynthia and Valdisera, Victor. 1986. *Women in the American Economy. U.S. Bureau of the Census Current Population Reports, Series P-23, No. 146*. Washington, D.C.: U.S. Government Printing Office.

Townson, Monica. 1993. *Tax Facts*. Ottawa: Canadian Advisory Council on the Status of Women.

United Nations. 1991. *The World's Women 1970-1990: Trends and Statistics*. New York: United Nations.

Vanier Institute on the Family. 1994. *Profiling Canada's Families*. Ottawa.

Waring, Marilyn 1988. *If Women Counted, A New Feminist Economics*. San Francisco: HarperCollins.

Waring, Marilyn. 1992. Decoding economic terms for real people. *Ms*. March/April:24-27.

Weitzman, Lenore. 1985. *The Divorce Revolution:The Unexpected Social and Economic Consequences for Women and Children in America*. New York: Free Press.

Zeidenberg, Jerry. 1993. Standoff at Siemens. *The Globe and Mail Report on Business*. December:63-69.